SEEING THE GROCERY STORE THROUGH SEINFELD EYES

R. SCOTT MURPHY

Visit mentalkickball.com to receive a free
Fun Pack plus the
weekly Fun Stories Universe humor newsletter

Dedication

To Jerry, Larry, Julia, Jason and Michael.
Congratulations on 30 years!

To Jenny, Jordan, Griffin, Curly, Jennifer and
Lt. Joe Bookman

To Schmoopie

In Loving Memory

Colonel Richard Dean Murphy (U.S. Army, retired)
(1939–2019)
Words can't express how grateful I am for everything you did for me, Dad.

Neil Peart
(1952–2020)
Love and life are deep...maybe as his skies are wide.

Sponsor

This book is made possible in part by the good folks at Kruger Industrial Smoothing.

Thank you.

Introduction

The IMDb summary for *Seinfeld* says, "The continuing misadventures of neurotic New York City stand-up comedian Jerry Seinfeld and his equally neurotic New York City friends." The key word here is "continuing." Even though the last episode aired on May 14, 1998, *Seinfeld's* stories remain humorous and very relevant.

Just as I was about to illustrate that relevance by writing that ESPN Sunday Night Baseball announcer Matt Vasgersian made a "Jerk Store" reference this season when then-St. Louis Cardinals' utility player Jedd Gyorko (pronounced "Jerk-oh") batted—something even wilder happened.

As I write the final chapters of this book in July 2019, the touchstone event of last night's 10-candidate Democratic Presidential Debate involved candidate Marianne Williamson injecting a *Seinfeld* moment into the evening. Williamson dropped a "yada, yada, yada" into the middle of one of her answers. The Internet lit up. *Seinfeld* hashtags flew around like airplanes. Williamson's "yada, yada, yada" made her the day's undisputed queen of meme. It's remarkable that more than 30 years since the inception of *Seinfeld*, a quote from it stole the show at a debate featuring a double-digit number of POTUS aspirants and watched by millions.

The first episode of *Seinfeld* aired on NBC on July 5, 1989. Where were you? Did you watch the first episode? Were you sleeping off a July 4th hangover? Were you even born? When did you become a *Seinfeld* fan? Why is the show still so popular?

In their book *Sitcoms*, Bloom and Vlastnik wrote that *Seinfeld* "mined comic gold from the little idiosyncrasies and annoyances of American life. These neurotic intricacies expose hilarious universal truths about the banality of life."

Escaping to Seinfeld World is a ticket to humorous adventures sans the restrictions of our normal lives. The characters are free to say things and do things that most of us just daydream about in the real world. We understand that if this were real life, the *Seinfeld* characters would not be upstanding citizens, but we love the wild ride all the same. The show takes real situations from the game of life, turns them upside down, and allows its characters to game the system.

Jerry Seinfeld and Larry David set the tone for the show by saying there would be "No hugging, no learning." This secret sauce set the show apart from previous TV shows, because it erased the expectations that had been established for creating and viewing sitcoms.

For many of us, that offered an opportunity to cut through normal TV show fluff and better connect with the show's content. The fact that we're still connecting 30 years later underscores the fact that, as *Seinfeld* fans, we all have our own unique *Seinfeld* story.

On July 5, 1989, I was finishing my sixth (and last) year of college. Before you label me a "Bluto Blutarsky," you should know that I was finishing my master's degree. Full disclosure, I did not know about *Seinfeld* when the first episode aired. This probably means I was studying (wink). The first *Seinfeld* episode I remember watching is

"The Library" in Season 3. It was hilarious, and a little surprising, to see how library cop (Lt. Joe Bookman) interrogated Jerry. My eyes flew wide open when he said, "What about that kid, sitting down, opening a book right now in a branch at the local library, and finding drawings of pee pees and wee wees?"

The episode featured high school flashbacks, wedgies, Kramer's forbidden love affair with the librarian, and the case of the missing book. There was nothing else like *Seinfeld* on primetime TV. I immediately started recording VHS copies of every episode—sometimes watching the latest episode several times before the next one aired. Many of my college friends knew I did this, and *Seinfeld* parties were frequent in my apartment. We sometimes ate cereal to mimic Jerry as we watched the show. Specifically, memories of the occasions when my friends tried to copy "The Kramer Entrance"—sliding, stumbling and shimmying into my apartment—still tickle a laugh out of me.

What are the details of your *Seinfeld* story? The following items might help you put all of the pieces together. On July 5, 1989, George H. W. Bush was President. A gallon of gas cost 97 cents. A postage stamp was 25 cents. The World Wide Web had not been born yet. As *Seinfeld* began to knock down TV boundaries, the stage was being set for the Berlin Wall to fall a few months later.

Music? Milli Vanilli topped the Billboard Hot 100 singles chart with "Baby Don't Forget My Number." Isn't pop music wonderful? I'd love to see the *Seinfeld* characters talk about Milli Vanilli. To complete the flashback picture I'm painting, *Batman*—the one with Michael Keaton, Jack Nicholson and Kim Basinger—topped the Box Office the week *Seinfeld* started.

We typically mark time in days, months, years, decades. I like to group the first 30 years of Seinfeld into a story called "My Seinfeld 30." The 30 years since the *Seinfeld* debut have seen me complete grad school, move from Missouri to Texas, get married, become the father of two children, work several different jobs, become an author, release eight books, and—to come full circle—send my first child to college.

It doesn't matter if you haven't kept track of the number of *Seinfeld* episodes you've watched, or if you know you have seen all 180 episodes many times. Either way, you experience your own heartfelt reaction from just the mention of *Seinfeld*, or one of its many popular catchphrases.

My wife and I have this "Jerry" bit that we've done for more than 20 years. It's usually a response to something silly, crazy, or ridiculous that happens in everyday life. The event happens, and one of us takes the lead, looks at the other and utters a surprised response in a Costanza-like voice. The line always ends with the word "Jerry." For example, *"I had no idea that you could pull the tape completely out of the tape measure, Jerry!"*

During the editing process of this book, my Google alert for *Seinfeld* went off. Yes, I have a Google alert set for *Seinfeld*. It was an announcement in *The Hollywood Reporter* that Netflix had landed the worldwide rights to the iconic sitcom in a five-year deal with Sony starting in 2021. Sources told *The Hollywood Reporter* that the new Seinfeld streaming pact is worth more than $500 million. It's no secret that Netflix is losing two of its most popular shows, *The Office* and *Friends*—so, in sports terms, they went out and signed the biggest free agent of them all.

To quote the show, "I'm busting!" My iTunes, DVR and DVD episodes aren't enough. I can't wait to be able to sit back and let Netflix feed me episode after episode of *Seinfeld!*

What follows is my version of a *Seinfeld* fan celebration. Thanks for coming along for the adventure. Say it with me, "Happy birthday, *Seinfeld!*"

Part I

The Calibration

Quick, think of your favorite *Seinfeld* episode. What pops into your head? "The Contest"? "The Soup Nazi"? "The Junior Mint"? Bet you can't stop at just one. Or ten. No matter what *Seinfeld* magic manifests in your memory, you have now successfully calibrated yourself to properly enjoy this book.

You see, *Seinfeld* is far more than a TV show; it's a state of mind.

Through Seinfeld Eyes

*I*t's the 30th anniversary of *Seinfeld*, the greatest sitcom of all time. It's a delicious opportunity for us, as *Seinfeld* fans, to say, "Sweet fancy Moses—let's celebrate!" As we honor this show, I challenge you to come up with more ways to take the *Seinfeld* fun to new places. For me, if there's a particular place that oozes with the craziness that begs for a *Seinfeld* way of seeing it, it's the grocery store.

Hello. I'm Scott Murphy. I live in Austin, Texas, and I have a confession to make. For the past year or so, I've been following people around in grocery stores, keeping a diary about their peculiar activities, and commenting about these actions in my mind using the voices of Jerry, Elaine, George, and Kramer from *Seinfeld*. Sometimes, other characters such as Frank Costanza, J Peterman, Newman, David Puddy, and Jackie Chiles work themselves into the mix. Who says book research has to be dull?

I'm going to share my long history of grocery store frivolity with you. I'll also share the incident that helped set the wheels in motion for this book. Then I'll crack open my grocery store diary and share the results with you. Believe me when I say that you're not going to believe some of the things I have seen.

Much of this fun is made possible by watching *Seinfeld*. Like millions of other folks, I've seen all 180 episodes of *Seinfeld*—most of them many times. In fact, I recently re-watched all of them to reacquaint myself with all of the madness so that I could properly appreciate it with you. Each *Seinfeld* episode is an old friend full of unique comedic tales and mischief. To put it mildly, the episodes resonate with me. I know they resonate with you as well, or you wouldn't be reading this book.

The bottom line? I've concluded that I've watched *Seinfeld* so many times that I've gained a heightened sense of observation of the wacky, the wild, and the wonderfully weird things in our world.

It's now my belief that I see the world through Seinfeld Eyes.

As a fan of the show, you see many things through Seinfeld Eyes too. You may not even realize it. It's a gift. A gift that lets you see a lot more humor in our world. When we open our Seinfeld Eyes, we can put our *Seinfeld* knowledge to practical use, and expand the ways in which people like us who love the show can enjoy it.

Having Seinfeld Eyes means your *Seinfeld* radar goes off nearly every day. It can happen at any time in any place. It might be at work, in traffic, or standing next to that guy in the movie theater who has a ridiculous way of eating nachos.

Soon, my diary overflowed with crazy things that my Seinfeld Eyes saw in the grocery store. I'll detail 30 of them in this book—30 years of *Seinfeld*, 30 items. It may change the way you look at the grocery store.

The fun doesn't stop there.

Later in this book, we'll spotlight several of the madcap characters, catchphrases, and all-round wackiness in the nine seasons of *Seinfeld*. I'll also give you a chance to try your hand at some *Seinfeld* quizzes, and put together a Seinfeld Fan Grocery List for you.

The official *Seinfeld* social media sites recently conducted a fan vote to decide the 30 favorite episodes. We'll check in on that and see what may have been missed. We'll also see how other media and fan sources ranked the episodes. In addition, we'll run down the top 30 episodes as voted by Fun Stories Universe, my fun-loving weekly newsletter group. We received votes from 17 countries in that poll!

Just as *Seinfeld* marched to its own drum, and blurred the line between the real world and the fictional world, the grocery store is a great place to see such different drummers in their natural habitat.

We'll start with The History of My Grocery Store Frivolity. Make sure your Seinfeld Eyes are open.

3

The History of My Grocery Store Frivolity

*F*or whatever reason, I like to elevate the grocery shopping experience by creating games, assigning points for clutch performances in various activities, humming along with in-store music, and pretty much turning the whole visit into my personal *Seinfeld*-influenced game show. Almost all of us have to go grocery shopping. Why not have some fun while we're at it, right?

My grocery store fun started some misty years ago during the 9th grade, when I frequently worked as a grocery bagger at the commissary at Carlisle Barracks in Pennsylvania. My dad, an Army Colonel, was attending the U.S. Army War College that year. I figured out later that it's a very prestigious thing to get selected to attend the U.S. Army War College, so I must mention how proud of you I am, dad!

At the commissary—that's the fancy military name for the grocery store—high school kids were invited to work as baggers during the weekends, the summer, and holidays. The hiring process had its own game show feel. You had to arrive at eight in the morning to be part of the "Bagger Lottery." Now that I'm an adult, that reporting time seems normal, but in those days, it seemed really early. In short, 30-40 kids would show up and try to land one of about 8-10 open spots.

Wiping the sleep from our eyes, we'd draw a folded piece of paper from a ceramic bowl. If it had a number on it, we got to work that day. I always wished there was a happy "da-da-da-da" trill, like in *The Price Is Right*, each time someone successfully drew a number. That would have completed the whole game show experience.

As an aspiring DJ and sportscaster, I often announced the whole process to the weary crowd. I remember my fellow 9th graders enjoying that type of thing. As a fan of the weekly *American Top 40* radio countdown show, my announcing often turned into a Casey Kasem-style Long Distance Dedication sendup.

> *"Now on AT 40, a song for a girl in Carlisle, Pennsylvania that hasn't pulled a number in 11 consecutive trips to the commissary. Yes, it's the Little River Band and their big hit Lonesome Loser."*

Like many teenage job experiences, the day was busy at times, while at other times there was room for a little creative fun. It was particularly enjoyable to point out idiosyncrasies in the customers and the full-time employees. One older (meaning he may have been 30 at the time) full-time commissary employee named "Will" always wore wristbands. I'd slap hands with him and call him "WBG" in a superhero voice. That just meant "Wrist Band Guy," but he enjoyed it, and I was not disrespecting him—I was just being the 9th grade version of enthusiastic.

One customer always had her dog with her. I don't think dogs were even allowed in the store. Her situation was different. It was my understanding that she was the wife of the second highest ranking officer on the Army Post—so maybe the regular rules did not apply to her. Her dog's name was "Fifi," and she would loudly call it about a dozen times during her shopping trips.

In a perfect world, I could spot her in the parking lot and begin randomly saying "Fifi" in a high-pitched voice before she entered the store. Several of us thought it would be particularly dangerous —and funny—if we could squeeze off a "Fifi" semi-yell while she was seemingly just out of earshot, shopping in the far corner of the commissary.

One day, however, I squeezed off a quick, shrill "Fifi," and she turned around and looked at me. I thought I was in trouble. Later, as luck would have it, it was my turn when her bags needed to be taken to the car. I was sure that I was in for a tongue lashing. Instead, "Mrs. Fifi" gave me a ten-dollar tip and said, "I love the energy you bring to the store. And even more than that, I love how much you love my dog, Fifi!" For a 9th grader, that's an extra good day!

This grocery store frivolity has endured (and sometimes grown out of control) for several decades since Fifi Day. It was not until recent years, however, when I was watching one of my favorite *Seinfeld* episodes, that I realized that not only did the TV show change my life, it also fueled the grocery store fun that I still enjoy to this day.

4

The Inspiration

Seinfeld celebrated the quirky things that happen in our everyday lives. It mined our universal experiences for humorous peculiarities. On a semi-chilly early November day, the inspiration for this book walked into the grocery store—and I saw him through Seinfeld Eyes.

The 50ish-year-old man came into the grocery store wearing red shorts with white stripes on the side, a headband, and older headphones with a long chord that hung down to his shorts. To put it mildly, his shorts were way too short. They looked as if they had walked right out of a 1970s NBA game. He had a little extra weight, so the shorts were even tougher for him to pull off as a fashion statement, or any other type of statement.

The first thing he did was walk over to the checkout stand and grab a bottled water from the cooler. Then he put the cold bottle to his forehead, cracked open the top, poured a bit of it in his hair, guzzled about half of it, and let out a loud "Aaaaaaaah." Of course, it was impossible not to observe him after that. Dude had only begun to make himself at home.

Even though I was wrapping up my shopping trip, I just had to swerve past the checkout line and follow this pied piper. I pushed my cart a safe distance behind him, so I could observe this unusual creature but not disturb it.

"The Inspiration" put on quite a show.

He pulled out a grocery cart, took his tennis shoes off, and put them in the basket; he was now walking on the floor in his bare feet —presumably to cool down from some type of strenuous workout. His stride was equal parts a Will Ferrell movie character and Steve Martin's "Wild and Crazy Guy" from *Saturday Night Live*. The whole store seemed to be his personal parade route.

Working out seemed to have made The Inspiration very hungry. He pulled out a glazed donut from the bakery display and chomped into it like a lion devouring its prey. The massive bites left glaze on his upper lip, and he didn't care.

Then The Inspiration drove his grocery cart around the store eating the donut, plus many of the available samples. He pointed at people who walked by him and said, in a voice garbled by food, "How are ya!" It wasn't a question; it was an exclamation.

Dude finished the water—and threw the bottle away. How was that going to work at the checkout stand?

Because he was wearing the headphones, he randomly hummed and sang the songs he was hearing—and what he was listening to was not the clean versions of the songs. There was a lot of "MF this," and "MF that" going on in those songs. Like a wild *Seinfeld* episode, The Inspiration was bending the perception—and the rules —of what normally happens in the grocery store.

I watched with wonder as he went from aisle to aisle, and then *it* happened. My mind started commenting about the activity—and all of the comments were made in *Seinfeld* voices.

Jerry Voice:
Will you look at that? He's made himself pretty comfortable.

George Voice:
I gotta tell ya. This all-you-can-eat lollygagger is making George angry.

Elaine Voice:
Oh…my…God. First he reached into the donuts—and pulled one out—now he's just eating everything like it's his birthday party.

Kramer Voice:
Giddy up! This happens all the time at the store where Bob Sacamano shops.

At that point, it occurred to me that I see things through Seinfeld Eyes pretty frequently, and almost as frequently, I comment about it in my head using these *Seinfeld* character voices. Even though I fully realized it on this day, I'm almost certain that I'd been doing it for quite some time before that.

5

30 Quick Grocery Store Facts

*E*arlier, we calibrated your mind to a *Seinfeld* frequency. We explored my history of grocery store frivolity and met the inspiration for my Seinfeld Eyes. As we prepare to crack open the grocery store diary, let's step up your grocery store knowledge with 30 quick grocery store facts.

The following statistics were compiled by the Time Use Institute, creditdonkey.com, IBISWorld, thebalancesmb.com, and the Food Marketing Institute.

1. HOW MUCH TIME WILL YOUR GROCERY SHOPPING TRIP TAKE?

The average grocery shopping trip takes 41 minutes.

Add 5-10 extra minutes if you run into The Talk Show Host—we'll talk about that later.

2. DO WOMEN OR MEN SPEND MORE TIME ON A GROCERY TRIP?

Women spend a little more time on their shopping trips, averaging 42 minutes. Men average 39 minutes.

3. HOW MANY TIMES DO WE SHOP PER WEEK? The average person takes 1.5 shopping trips per week. *That's kind of like having 2.4 kids.*

4. HOW MANY HOURS DO WE SHOP A YEAR?

The average person spends more than 53 hours per year in the grocery store. That's more than two days.

Imagine spending two straight days at the store. That sounds like a great reality show.

5. DOES IT TAKE LONGER TO SHOP ON THE WEEKEND?

If you shop on Saturday or Sunday, you'll spend an average of seven more minutes per trip.

As Billie Eilish would say, "Duh."

6. WHAT DAY IS THE MOST POPULAR FOR GROCERY SHOPPING?

Approximately 41 million Americans choose Saturday as their day to shop.

I think I've seen all of them, at some point, while standing in the grocery store line.

7. ON AN AVERAGE DAY, HOW MANY AMERICANS HEAD TO THE GROCERY STORE? On an average day, 32 million Americans head to the grocery store. That's 1 in 7 adults who are shopping at any given time.

. . .

8. WHICH DAYS HAVE LESS SHOPPERS?

If you're able to shop on Mondays or Tuesdays, you'll avoid the biggest crowds. Those days average 29 million shoppers (only).

9. WHAT IS PEAK TRAFFIC TIME ON THE WEEKEND?

On weekends, it is between 11 am and noon.

10. WHAT IS PEAK TRAFFIC TIME ON WEEKDAYS? On weekdays, peak traffic time is between 4 pm and 5 pm. *I'm insanely jealous of all of those folks who can be done with work and hit the store by 4 pm.*

11. DESPITE MANY OTHER OPTIONS, WHAT PERCENTAGE OF SHOPPERS STILL MAKE TRADITIONAL SUPERMARKETS THEIR MAIN CHOICE FOR FOOD SHOPPING?

83% of shoppers make traditional supermarkets their go-to choice for edible purchases.

12. WHAT PERCENTAGE OF GROCERY SHOPPERS GO TO MORE THAN ONE STORE TO GET WHAT THEY NEED?

More than 40% of shoppers say they go to more than one store to get all the things they need.

13. WHAT PERCENTAGE OF WOMEN MAKE A GROCERY LIST?

69% of women say they make a list before going shopping.

. . .

14. WHAT PECENTAGE OF MEN MAKE A GROCERY LIST?

52% of men say they make a list before going shopping. *To me, this means women are more efficient shoppers, because they are more likely to make a list.*

15. WHAT PERCENTAGE OF WOMEN USE COUPONS?

57% of women say they use coupons.

16. WHAT PERCENTAGE OF MEN USE COUPONS? 41% of men say they use coupons.

17. HOW MANY SUPERMARKETS ARE THERE IN THE UNITED STATES?

There are nearly 38,000 supermarkets in the United States. *If you had one year, how many of them could you visit? Bam! There's another reality show idea.*

18. HOW MANY OF THESE ARE CONVENTIONAL GROCERY STORES?

70% are conventional grocery stores, with the other 30% being supercenters, gourmet stores, warehouse clubs, and military commissaries.

It's also funny to note that in the movie industry, the commissary is the place where you eat in the studio lot—not the place where you shop.

19. WHAT'S THE AVERAGE AGE FOR ADULT GROCERY SHOPPERS IN THE UNITED STATES?

The average age of adult grocery shoppers is 44. The average age for female shoppers is slightly higher at 47. *The average age of the person who's usually in front of me in the checkout line is 87.*

. . .

20. WHAT'S THE AVERAGE WEEKLY GROCERY BILL FOR MULTI-PERSON HOUSEHOLDS? Multi-person households spend an average of $118 per week on groceries.

21. WHAT'S THE AVERAGE WEEKLY GROCERY BILL FOR SINGLE SHOPPERS?

Single shoppers spend an average of $60 per week on groceries.

22. WHAT ARE THE TOTAL SUPERMARKET SALES IN THE UNITED STATES?

Supermarket sales in the United States topped $682 billion in 2017.

23. WHAT IS THE AVERAGE NET PROFIT FOR A GROCERY STORE?

You might be surprised to find out that the average net profit for a grocery store is just 1.1%.

I think that's why a lot of them did away with those little twist-ties for the plastic bags in the fruit section. Every penny counts!

24. WHAT IS THE MEDIAN WEEKLY SALES AMOUNT PER SUPERMARKET?

The median weekly sales amount per supermarket is $406,000.

25. WHAT IS THE AVERAGE NUMBER OF ITEMS STOCKED IN A SUPERMARKET?

According to 2017 statistics, the average number of items stocked in a supermarket is 30,098.

. . .

26. HOW COMMON IS ONLINE GROCERY SHOPPING?

The number is increasing, but right now just 3% of shoppers say they purchase their groceries via the Internet. *If you are reading this book a few years after its publication date, you are undoubtedly laughing at this number.*

27. WHAT PERCENTAGE OF OUR HOUSEHOLD DISPOSABLE INCOME DO WE SPEND ON GROCERIES?

On average, we spend 5.6% of our disposable income on grocery purchases.

28. WHAT PERCENTAGE OF SHOPPERS DO ALL THE SHOPPING FOR THEIR HOUSEHOLD? 68% of grocery shoppers say they're solely responsible for doing all the shopping for their family.

29. WHAT'S THE OLDEST GROCERY STORE IN AMERICA?

According to onlyinyourstate.com, the oldest family-owned grocery store in America is Doud's Market on Mackinac Island in Michigan. It opened in 1884.

Extra trivia: Chester A. Arthur was President of the United States in 1884.

30. WHAT ARE THE TEN TOP-SELLING GROCERY AND SUPERMARKET CHAINS?

According to 2018 statistics, the top ten are as follows:
• #1: The Kroger Company
• #2: Albertson's Companies, Limited
• #3: Publix Supermarkets, Inc.
• #4: H. E. Butt Grocery Company (H-E-B)
• #5: Whole Food Markets

- #6: Southeastern Grocers, LLC
- #7: Hyvee, Inc.
- #8: Gant Eagle, Inc.
- #9: Wegmans Food markets, Inc.
- #10: WinCo Foods LLC

Part II—The Diary

Without further ado, let's celebrate 30 years of *Seinfeld* by taking a look at my diary of 30 things I've seen at the grocery store through Seinfeld Eyes.

Let the insanity begin!

1

The Marty McFlys

$\mathcal{I}$n the 43rd episode of *Seinfeld* (Season 4, Episode 3) titled "The Pitch," Kramer drinks expired milk and vomits on George's new girlfriend, Susan Ross. Sadly, that won't be the worst thing that happens to Susan on the show. I call the folks in our first diary entry "The Marty McFlys." They work very hard to greatly reduce the chances of Kramer's misfortune ever befalling them.

By way of reminder, Marty McFly (played by Michael J. Fox) is the main character in the *Back To The Future* movies.

Have you seen any Marty McFlys in your store? If not, then I'm sorry to inform you that you're probably one yourself. In fact, full disclosure, I'm one of them as well. I'm talking about people who are constantly looking for the milk container with the last possible date in(to) the future stamped on it.

You don't even need a flux capacitor to go (back) to the future in this grocery store milk game. You just need a keen eye and a reasonable reach. It's almost like playing a sport, or a numbers game that is easier to win than the lottery, or even Bingo.

I like to say, "It's McFly Time," when I reach the milk section of the grocery store. Recently, I felt great joy and excitedly remarked to my wife that we had scored a "Plus 5." This meant I had gained five extra days of Jerry Seinfeld–inspired cereal enjoyment just by ignoring the milk containers in the front row and grabbing one located three levels deeper in the display case. She doesn't enjoy being around me when I grab the milk. This is especially true if I need to use the bottom of the grocery store cooler as a temporary stair in order to retrieve a Plus 3, Plus 4, or Plus 5.

The whole process is usually an excuse for her to grab something in a nearby aisle. All in all, I'm sure she enjoys the extra days of milk consumption, but she does not want to watch while they are being made possible.

Yes, there are dates on most things—eggs, lunchmeat, peanut butter, chips, meat, and so on, but milk expiration dates seem to draw the most scrutiny—and the most Marty McFlys.

I sometimes feel a bit guilty about the possibility of milk being wasted when I turn into Marty McFly and go all back-to-the-future back-of-the-cooler on my milk date. I'm sure you hate this practice if you produce the packed milk—or run the local grocery store, convenience store, or drug store that sells milk. I'd feel really bad if I had to watch them throw away milk that had been perfectly good several days earlier, but I've never seen anybody preach against this practice. Maybe the National Dairy Council needs to produce a sad PSA about wasted milk.

I believe the solution to the Marty McFly milk problem might lie in pricing the milk containers that have earlier expiration dates a little lower than the ones with extra days. I know, this is probably too much work compared to the benefit to the store, but it would make me pause and think. I'd stand there and wonder if I could eat enough cereal, dunk enough cookies, etc. during the lesser time period to justify saving 10-15 cents. I'm thinking I would often go for the savings.

During my several decades of milk expiration date upgrading, I had never seen the Spider-Man version of Marty McFly—until a few weeks ago. I had already traded up four days and was pretty pleased about it. I stood there holding the milk like it was a Dundee Award.

The guy after me, however, was a crawler. Spider McFly was

lean and wiry. He had spotted an even better date on the top shelf that's located way in the back of the cooler. Without warning, he physically climbed inside the milk cooler—I'm talking all of him—to grab the precious milk carton with the date the most further into the future.

I hadn't seen anything this athletic since Michael Phelps swam in his last Olympics. I just stood there and smiled. I almost clapped, but I didn't think my wife, or Spider McFly himself, would want this extra attention.

When we made eye contact, I got that George Costanza vibe from him, from when George had falsely bragged that he was an architect who had designed a local building—and it really hadn't taken that long. Spider McFly gave me a wry smile and went on his way. I knew then that he'd be doing this again soon. I wish I could see it again. I wish all of his antics would be available on pay-per-view.

SEINFELD FAN FUN

CHARACTER MOST LIKELY TO BE A MARTY McFLY
Kramer

CHARACTER LEAST LIKELY TO BE A MARTY McFLY
Jerry

CHARACTER THAT DRINKS THE MOST MILK
Jerry—and it's not even close

CHARACTER THAT PAINTS HIS FACE BEFORE HE DRINKS MILK
David Puddy

CHARACTER THAT COULD DO THE BEST JOB ADVERTISING MILK

Jackie Chiles—*"It's delicious, nutritious, scrumpdillyicious. Who told you it's not as healthy as your grandparents thought?"*

CHARACTER THAT MIGHT ENJOY A GLASS OF MILK WHILE EATING A BLOCK OF CHEESE THE SIZE OF A CAR BATTERY
George

REAL WORLD FUN

In the *Seinfeld* tradition of poring over the minutia of daily events, here's some additional information about this first item.

- Madison.com says the typical American consumes 276 pounds of dairy a year, including nearly 199 pounds of fluid milk.
- Brandongaille.com says the average American cow produces more than 22,000 pounds of milk over the course of a lifetime.
- Marty McFly had many aliases in the *Back To The Future* movies. Lorraine thought his name was Calvin Klein. Marty calls himself Darth Vader in the first movie. In the third movie, Marty claims to be Clint Eastwood. In the Back To The Future game, the fun continues. Marty uses three aliases: Sonny Crockett, Harry Callahan, and Michael Corleone.
- If you're ever asked to set a flux capacitor, make sure you set it for 1.21 Gigawatts. It's been speculated that using that setting gives about the same energy as found in 26 gallons of gasoline.
- Dumpsters.com reports that supermarkets throw away 43 billion pounds of food every year.
- Emily Broad Leib, Director, Food Law and Policy Clinic (Harvard Law School), says the industry standard for date labeling on milk is generally 21 to 24 days after pasteurization. She says the date label on milk, like on

most foods, is generally meant to indicate quality rather than safety. Because pasteurization kills harmful pathogens, milk is safe and generally still good well past the date.

- However, my nose automatically senses a sour smell if I take a whiff of a milk container past its expiration date.
- One of the scariest things for me is when someone smells milk, makes a face, and then asks me to smell it. I always tell them that I will go with their verdict on the situation.

2

The Angry Sea(Crests)

$\mathcal{F}$or some time, I have called anybody that gets on the microphone in a store "Seacrest." Of course, this is a reference to Ryan Seacrest, host of *American Idol*, host of morning radio and TV, host of the *American Top 40* radio show, host of *New Year's Rockin' Eve*... you get the point—he's very good at talking into a microphone.

The store's PA system gives birth to many types of grocery store Seacrests.

SCARED SEACREST
This person doesn't want to be on the microphone, but they have been asked to do it. They stumble over their words, put their mouth too close to the microphone, and say, "We need more checkers at the frosh registers—I mean front registers, just please come right now."

TOO VERBOSE, J PETERMAN SEACREST
"The delicious, butter-basted baked bread just came out of the artisan oven and has been gently snuggled in our environment-friendly packages that are safe for recycling once you have enjoyed

our mouth-watering, Kansas-grown bread. Each loaf will make you smile, nourish your soul, and bring your family closer together. Get one now while supplies last. They're conveniently located in the finely crafted wooden barrel near the front register."

BAD RAPPER SEACREST
(DOING A BAD BEAT BOX)
Boys and girls, women and men
It's sick to see you in our store again.
Take a minute and check the app
To see exactly what's happ—ening.
We appreciate your Benjamins, we appreciate your time
Head to register now if you want a short line.

I get the feeling that Lil' Wayne or Jay-Z could have pulled this one off, but the high school guy dissing these lines lacked attitude and stood too far from the mic. It was especially funny to see an older lady wearing a fur coat on a 65-degree day make a face and shake her head in outrage the whole time Bad Rapper Seacrest was doing his thing.

All this grocery store Seacrest stuff made for great diary entries. It simultaneously amused me and reminded me of the days that I worked at Kmart and announced Blue Light specials on the microphone all day. Those are stories for another day.

THE ANGRY SEA-CREST
I had just passed the seafood section and given a "hey man" and head nod to the guy wearing a college T-shirt that worked there. I had no idea he was about to take The Seacrest Game to another level—an incredibly fun *Seinfeld* level!

The microphone clicks on and this is what I hear:

"Hey shoppers, we have a great deal on freshly caught shrimp and crab legs in our seafood aisle. Let me tell you about it. I got on the boat early this morning, and the sea was angry, my friends. It

was like an old man trying to send back soup in a deli. Not our deli
—another, far less satisfying deli."

Of course, he had me at "the sea was angry, my friends," ("The
Marine Biologist," Season 5, Episode 14), but the fun continued.

He said, "I knew I had to wear my pirate shirt ("The Puffy
Shirt," Season 5, Episode 2) in order to survive and get this deal to
you. I got about 50 feet from the crabs and shrimp, and suddenly I
realized they were being guarded by a whale. I tell you he was 10
stories high if he was a foot. As if sensing my presence, he let out a
great bellow. I said, 'Easy, big fella!' And then, as I watched him
struggle, I realized that he wanted me to be aware that you needed a
better deal on your seafood than any other place in town. Out of
nowhere, a huge tidal wave lifted me, tossed me like a cork, and I
found myself right on top of the best seafood opportunities in the
state. They were all over me. It was like Rocky 1. I had tears
streaming down my face. You'll be the titleist in your home when
you bring home our jumbo shrimp and Alaskan King Crag Leg
deals. Tell them George sent you!"

I was so overwhelmed with joy that he had not only just gone for
it and performed well, but he had also worked one of the greatest
moments in *Seinfeld* history into his speech. In fact, Jerry Seinfeld
himself has called George's speech at the end of the episode "The
Marine Biologist" the sitcom's funniest scene.

From two aisles away, I started clapping. I was alone for about 5
seconds, but that didn't slow me down. I proudly continued clapping. Soon, I heard more clapping and then a loud whistle. A lady
yelled, "*Seinfeld*!" A couple of other people looked confused, but
that's just the way these random *Seinfeld* events shape out.

I flipped the cart around, headed for the seafood aisle, and spontaneously purchased a pound of jumbo shrimp that had not been on
my list. It would be funnier to say that I don't even enjoy shrimp,
but I do. Four other people formed a line behind me. We all praised
the Angry Seacrest performance. Full disclosure, I also started the
round of David Puddy high-fives that, eventually, everyone
gave him.

I've said it before, and I'll say it again, mix in some *Seinfeld* with almost any situation, and watch the magic happen!

SEINFELD FAN FUN

CHARACTER MOST LIKELY TO MAKE GROCERY STORE ANNOUNCEMENTS
Kramer

CHARACTER MOST LIKELY TO BE IRRITATED BY GROCERY STORE ANNOUNCEMENTS
George

CHARACTER MOST LIKELY TO CRITIQUE A GROCERY STORE ANNOUNCER
Jerry

CHARACTER MOST LIKELY TO DANCE BADLY IF A GROCERY STORE ANNOUNCER BEAT BOXES THE MESSAGE
Elaine

CHARACTER MOST LIKELY TO BET ON THINGS PEOPLE ANNOUNCE IN THE STORE
Earl Haffler

REAL WORLD FUN

- In an interview with the Atlanta Journal-Constitution newspaper, Ryan Seacrest's mother, Constance Marie said, "Instead of playing with G.I. Joes or Cowboys and Indians, Ryan would always have a little microphone and do shows in the house."
- *Bonus fact:* Many consider Constance Marie Seacrest to

be Taylor Swift's doppelganger. Google her pictures for yourself and see if you agree.

- According to tonsoffacts.com, Seacrest's first time in the spotlight was in fourth grade. He performed the singing role of King Winter in a school musical, and he forgot his lines.
- According to seafoodhealthfacts.org, in 2017, U.S. fishermen made commercial landings of 9.9 billion pounds valued at $5.4 billion at ports in the 50 states.
- According to careerexplorer.com, the average salary of a marine biologist is $32,000. In the same survey, job satisfaction is rated as "very high".
- The Bureau of Labor Statistics lists the median pay for marine biologists as $62,290, saying marine biologists are often classified together with all zoologists and wildlife biologists.

3

The Superhero Of Savings

---

*V*ery late in the process of writing this book, I experienced an "instant classic" event. It made me rework the order of these chapters, bump an item that was supposed to be included, and remark in my diary that this was one of the most bizarre things I've seen in the grocery store through Seinfeld Eyes.

This is because the lady ringing up my groceries was so animated and off the wall. Plus, she had this whole routine that was different than anything else I'd ever seen before at the grocery store. Let's call her "Annie"—that's short for "animated"—to make the story more fun.

It's bonus fun if you hum or play the song "Smooth Criminal" by Michael Jackson as you read this story. No, Grocery Store Annie didn't steal anything, and nobody was attacked (as is the case with the song). In short, there is a section of the song that keeps playing in my mind, "Annie are you OK? Annie are you OK, will you tell us that you're OK?"

If you've ever seen the music video, Michael Jackson does an anti-gravity lean in it that seems almost impossible. Due to selective retention, I now picture Grocery Store Annie doing that same anti-gravity lean as this next sequence unfolded.

Everything started out in a normal way. The scene begins as Annie's almost finished scanning my grocery items…

SCOTT: And before I forget, I'm proud to report that I have four whole coupons. Let the savings begin!

At that point, I hand her the coupons and her face lights up like I've dropped money into a video game console.

ANNIE (SCREAMING LIKE MEG RYAN'S CHARACTER DURING THE DELI SCENE IN "WHEN HARRY MET SALLY"): I'll save you! I'll save all of you coupons! This store and this city are all about savings, and I'm going to save all of you. S-A-V-E!

SCOTT: I had no idea that you have such superpowers…

Annie looks at the first coupon, tosses down the other coupons, and starts rummaging through the items for Cheez-Its. She makes flying noises and lands the coupon for Cheez-Its on the Cheez-Its box as she continues with the sound effects.

ANNIE: Boom! Pow! I'll save you! Yes! There's some savings for you, Mr. Cheez-Its! (SHE SCANS THE COUPON) You're saved! You're saved! You're saved! It's all going to be OK! Savings have been registered! Crisis averted!

Here, I should note that the teenage guy bagging the groceries does not even move a muscle at this performance. So obviously, this happens a lot, and he has seen this routine many times. Like it or hate it, the bit is out of the ordinary and certainly brightens up a dull day. It makes me wonder why the grocery store hasn't considered using her OTT bit in one of its commercials or on its social media.

SCOTT: That's amazing. You're like Avengers and the Justice League all rolled up into one.

But Annie's lost in saving the world. She is oblivious to my comments and looking down at the next coupon.

ANNIE: Oh my, we need to get to the pizza right away. It's a big job. We're going to need both pizzas to get the 50 cents in savings.

With that, she pulls the two pizzas that had already been bagged out of one of my orange grocery bags. Annie looks both ways, seemingly for bad guys, and then smacks each pizza with the coupon.

ANNIE: Kapow! Pow! Pow Wow! Oh my Lord it's so much tougher when we have to save two at a time, but we did it. You're both saved. The savings are registered (SCANS THE COUPON). It's another pizza miracle! There will be savings with every slice you eat! Every slice! Savings! Think of all of the proud pepperonis!

SCOTT: I almost got four pizzas, but sadly I saw it was "limit 2" on the savings. Will you act like you don't know me if I come back later and buy two more? Is that allowed?

. . .

Again, Annie is lost in her own world.

ANNIE: Peanuts! Where are the peanuts? You need to be saved!

The guy behind me in line starts to chuckle as I simultaneously realize that when Annie said "peanuts," it sounded a lot like "penis." Was she doing this on purpose? I decided she was not, but Bagger Guy and I both started making TV show Jerry faces each time she uttered the word "peanuts."

ANNIE: 75 cents off peanuts today! Peanuts! Peanuts, where are you? We can do it! I'll save you, Peanuts!

Once again, the item has already been bagged. She spots the peanuts in one of the orange bags and dumps all of the items out to get to it. Bagger Guy is not real pleased that she is creating more work for him.

But impervious, Annie makes a flying noise and then smacks the coupon on top of the jar of peanuts like she is giving it a high five.

ANNIE: You're saved! You're saved, peanuts! We have saved the peanuts! My work with peanuts is done. Go into the world, peanuts! More savings!

At this, the guy behind me loses it and breaks into an alarmingly weird chuckle. We can only hope that he does not also have a coupon for peanuts.

· · ·

Now, I am trying to remember the fourth and final coupon. I am also sad that I haven't been more resourceful and used more coupons. Now, the last coupon was for…

ANNIE: Coffee! Coffee! The only thing better than coffee is saving money on coffee! I'll save you, coffee.

I don't have the heart to tell her that I don't even drink coffee. The coffee is for my wife, but it is a full $3.00 off. This is sure to get Annie's attention. I also think that just this part of her grocery store routine would be a fun clip for Jerry Seinfeld's "Comedians In Cars Getting Coffee" show.

ANNIE: It's almost like winning the lottery! Three dollars off your coffee! I'm gonna save you that money! Full speed ahead for coffee savings! Choo-choo!

With that, she dumps another bag to get to the large Keurig-style coffee box. Bagger Guy is beaten by now. He simply drops his head and waits to bag again.

ANNIE: There you are! What are we doing? Saving! Money! On! Coffee!

She picks up the box, gives it a hug—for several seconds—and then pats the coupon against the box. Then she scans the coupon, closes her eyes and takes a deep breath.

. . .

ANNIE: Three dollars saved! Three dollars saved! My work here is complete!

Just as I am smiling again, she turns off the animated personality, gives me a blank stare, and says, in a fairly quiet voice…

ANNIE: Please swipe your card now for payment.

Animated Annie's gone. Normal Annie's back.

Of course, she wasn't as much fun. I swiped my card. She said "Thank you for shopping with us today" and turned to ring up the next person. As I looked around, there were now about six or seven people in my line, even though some other lines only had one or two people.

It was all kind of enchanting until the guy behind me spoke. I'm 99% certain that he was wondering whether she was this animated in other situations. He gave her a near-stalker smile and said, "You're pretty cute. I want the same treatment for my coupons."

Annie, wherever you are, I hope you're OK.

SEINFELD FAN FUN

MOST LIKELY TO ACT LIKE ANNIE
Kramer

MOST LIKELY TO WANT TO DATE ANNIE

George

FUNNIEST PERSON TO PAIR WITH ANNIE
Frank Costanza

MOST CONFUSING PERSON TO PAIR WITH ANNIE
J Peterman

PERSON WE SHOULD KEEP AWAY FROM ANNIE
THE MOST
Newman

SECRETLY DATED ANNIE
Cousin Jeffrey

HOW MANY DATES JERRY WOULD LAST BEFORE
WANTING TO BREAK UP WITH ANNIE?

Less than one—it would be like a referee stopping a boxing match
right after it begins because one person is endangering the other
person.

REAL WORLD FUN

BONUS INFORMATION

- After mentioning Michael Jackson's "Smooth Criminal"
  song and calling the woman "Annie" in my story, I
  learned a lot more about Annie.
- Jackson's chorus refrain, "Annie, are you OK?," was
  inspired by Resusci Anne, a dummy used in CPR

training courses. CPR trainees learn to say "Annie, are you OK" while practicing resuscitation on the dummy.

- You can buy CPR Manikins on Amazon. One adult and infant CPR Manikin set I saw cost $408. Another CPR Manikin set had two adults and two infants and cost $724. There was also an adult 4-pack of CPR Manikins for $556. Finally, I saw an 8-pack of CPR Manikins that featured 4 adults and 4 infants. It cost $1,529.
- All joking aside, it's very helpful to know CPR. You can visit redcross.org to see CPR steps and find a CPR class near you.

4

The Fruit Fondlers

*I*n the *Seinfeld* episode "The Mango," (Season 5, Episode 1) Kramer gets banned from Joe's Grocery for his intense interactions/encounters with fruit. That's the inspiration for this next diary entry.

The fruit section may have more going on than any other section in the store. Some of it is fun. Some of it is fancy. Some of it is just plain weird. I think this is because, at any given time, people are engaging all of their five basic senses in the aisles of the fruit section. By way of reminder, those senses are sight, hearing, smell, taste, and touch.

Often when you're in the store, you see people lovingly handling fruit. I call them The Fruit Fondlers. Yes, they're very serious about their fruit. There was a guy with a peach in one hand and a lemon in the other. I kept wondering why he chose these two particular items as Steve Miller's "Really love your peaches..." and Led Zeppelin's "Squeeze my lemon..." simultaneously played in my head.

The Fruit Fondlers category has a lot of subcategories. This includes The Grape Faces. These people have to taste a grape before buying a bunch. You can often see these people taste a grape and make that happy face. During this study, however, I also saw a lady eat a grape and then make a terrible face as she shook her head and said, "Ewwww!" in a particularly frightening voice.

Next, there are The Banana Blenders. These people pick the best bananas from different stalks and shove them in a plastic bag to make their own stalk of the best. It surprised me the first time I saw it. By the third time I saw it, I figured I'd missed some Food Network show that every other shopper knew about months ago.

If you've ever uttered the phrase, "I'd like to tap that," you might be one of The Watermelon Tappers. Many people think they have a special talent that lets them know which melons are the best by simply tapping them. Other people are aspiring musicians and tap the watermelon different ways to make different sounds. I'm shocked at the absence of an actual mix song featuring grocery store melons.

As I write this, my wife just confessed to being part of The Avocado Squeezers. She agrees with the *Seinfeld* episode that says the harder ones are better. She's very serious about her avocados. One of her friends brings them back from across the border when she visits family in Laredo. Supposedly those are some of the best ones. As you can tell, avocados are not my thing. I'm sorry I can't join you avocado lovers in this current avocado toast craze.

The other week, I saw a man hold up two oranges side by side. It looked a bit erotic as he stared them down and turned them sideways with his hands like he was adjusting an old radio dial. Another lady was smelling the peaches. Not once or twice. She must have smelled them four times. Maybe she just likes that temporary aromatic peach high?

Tomatoes are The Mystery Fruit—not that there's anything wrong with that—because lots of people still don't realize they are a fruit. I heard a kid say to his mom, "How can tomatoes be a fruit if they're in my spaghetti?" That's almost exactly how I felt when I first found out this "tomato fruit" mystery years ago. I tried to get my mom to count eating pizza as part of my fruit intake because of the tomato sauce. Readers, that idea did not receive Mom Approval.

I'd like to proclaim pineapples The Cactus of the Fruit Section.

Truth be told, I don't like handling them. I always do it incorrectly. Call me crazy, pineapple connoisseurs, but I'm OK with getting my pineapples out of a can. But I do draw the line at heavy syrup in my canned pineapples. Who enjoys that?

For me, a coconut always conjures memories of "Gilligan's Island" episodes—and of Dawn Wells as Mary Ann. She would always make coconut cream pies on the show. Random thought, but does anybody remember duck pin bowling? I've always thought that a coconut could double as the ball at a duck pin bowling alley.

We haven't even mentioned the apples yet—the source of the original sin. We used to have medium red apples and large red apples in our store. Now, they are all large. Was there a revolution? Did the medium ones get shipped somewhere else because everything is bigger in Texas? I always get the red ones. Can the yellow and green ones even be trusted? Maybe I need to expand my horizons.

It's worth an entire trip to the store just to observe The Fruit Fondlers. Go around noon on a Saturday to see a large number of them. Most of them will be doing Fruit Fondler things—and loving it!

SEINFELD FAN FUN

CHARACTER MOST LIKELY TO BE A FRUIT FONDLER
Kramer

CHARACTER LEAST LIKELY TO BE A FRUIT FONDLER
Jerry

CHARACTER THAT'S SECRETLY PRETTY GOOD AT
THROWING FRUIT
Elaine

IF WE NEEDED ONE CHARACTER THAT APPEARED ON
SEINFELD FOR A LIFE-OR-DEATH FRUIT THROWING

OPPORTUNITY TO SAVE THE UNIVERSE, I WOULD
CHOOSE…
Keith Hernandez

WHO WOULD WIN THE ALL-STAR FRUIT THROWING
COMPETION BETWEEN LLOYD BRIDGES AND FRANK
COSTANZA?
Lloyd Bridges, of course

REAL WORLD FUN

What fruit do you buy the most? What do you think are the best-selling fruits? Stop a second and guess the top three.

This is the part where you think for a second.

This is the part where you think, "Alright, Scott, get on with it, already."

According to the Produce Marketing Association, these are the 10 best-selling fruits (based on 2018 statistics):

- #10: Pineapples—*not a bad ranking for a fruit I usually eat out of a can*
- #9: Peaches—*I thought this one might be a little higher*
- #8: Blueberries—*It's fun to see if you can eat a whole container of them in one sitting*
- #7: Lemons—*I'd put this one closer to #10*
- #6: Watermelons—*They'd be higher if it weren't for all the thumping*
- #5: Oranges—*I'm thinking we need a re-count. Only #5?*
- #4: Strawberries—*I'm very surprised they snuck past oranges*
- #3: Grapes— *I wonder if grocery store consumption got counted in this total*
- #2: Apples—*I'm thinking if stores carried more medium-sized ones, then apples would have made it to #1*

- #1: Bananas—*This is a surprise to me. I thought it would be apples. Watch out for The Banana Blenders!*

After a countdown like that, I feel like I need to pay tribute to Casey Kasem and say, "Keep your feet on the ground and keep reaching for the fruit." Of course, Casey actually said, "Keep reaching for the stars."

5

The Grocery Store Schmoopies

*R*ight off the top, I must tell you that my wife Jenny and I have somewhat different opinions about the romantic pet name "Schmoopie." I think the term is hilarious. I once had a fantasy football team named "Schmoopie's Revenge." I'd give our pets that name if she'd agree to it.

But, she won't. It's probably because I always need to say "Schmoopie" at least 6-7 times in a row in a silly voice each time I think about it. If I'm watching the *Seinfeld* episode ("The Soup Nazi," Season 7, Episode 6), I need to say "Schmoopie" about 10-15 times. At that point, she has had enough Schmoopie for a long time. I sympathize with her feelings, but saying "Schmoopie" is kind of like eating potato chips—more is definitely better.

As I began taking notes in my grocery store diary, I made sure to watch for Schmoopie-style schmoozing. The first one I heard was "Moon Pie." There were many uses of "Honey." "Baby Cakes" got a few entries. "Hot Stuff" was pretty popular. Later in the process, I heard "Snug," which I assume is short for "Snuggles." Have to admit that's kind of cool. An older gentleman called his wife "Booty." Is that even OK in today's world? I'm not sure that qualifies as a term of endearment here.

Observing was not enough. I needed to do research.

Once again, the Internet proved to be a helpful friend. Relationship therapist Jamie Turndorf, PhD, says, "Using nicknames and made-up language is an easy way to inject positive communication in everyday life. In fact, it's probably the single easiest thing you can do to keep your relationship going strong." (Jezebel.com)

According to Leslie Goldman of *Women's Health*, couples that create their own romantic language—complete with annoying voices, code words, and stupid nicknames—have a better chance of being satisfied with their partners.

Goldman also notes that such amorous nicknames and in-jokes can serve as a means to de-escalate tension during rough patches, and that in-jokes serve as a means to reinforce positive memories and keep couples close.

"Whether he calls you Rodeo, after the horseback-riding trip you took on your first anniversary, or you call him Speed Racer, for the time he drove 90 mph to get you to the airport on time, the names are a way of tracking your romantic history," she writes.

That's my new Schmoopie strategy with my wife. When I say it, I am tracking our romantic history.

Want to quickly locate other fans to strike up a *Seinfeld* conversation during a multi-hour delay at the airport? Simply say the word Schmoopie a few times.

Schmoopie is also a great *Seinfeld* fan test. If somebody says they are a fan of the show, slip Schmoopie into the conversation. In my estimation, you are not a true *Seinfeld* fan if you don't know about Schmoopie.

All of these nicknames became so fascinating that I put together a fun list of 50+ nicknames I call "Schmoops" that I gleaned from several sites: pairedlife.com, zoosk.com, and nicknames.com. Thank you to all of these sites for some fascinating reading. For fans of "The Bubble Boy" (Season 4, Episode 7) episode of *Seinfeld*, it'll also be fun to note that Schmoops rhymes with Moops.

As you read the list, do it in your silliest Seinfeld Schmoopie voice. Say the word first, then right after saying it, change voices and say, "No, you're Baby Cakes," or whatever word you are on at the time. If you go through the list more than once, you're sure to notice that it gets funnier each time. Add some beer, and these Schmoops might carry a whole party.

Enjoy!

SCHMOOPS

- Aphrodite—*Do you think people really say this, or did someone just think it would look good on a list?*
- Baby Cakes—*No, you're Baby Cakes. Remember to read these in your Silly Jerry Voice.*
- Beef Cakes
- Beef Jerky—*Be careful, this could easily be turned upside down into a Jerk Store reference.*
- Big Bird
- Bond Girl
- Bunny
- Care Bear
- Champ
- Chief
- Chubby Bunny—*Be very careful with this one.*
- Cookie Monster—*50+ years of Sesame Street makes for great nicknames!*
- Cuddle Cakes
- Donut
- Dream Boat
- Elf
- Fluffy—*There are so many directions you can go with this one…*
- Fly Guy
- Gumdrop
- Gummy Bear
- Hot Boy
- Hot Buns
- Hot Lips—*There are probably a dozen more Schmoops that could start with "hot."*

- Hubba Bubba
- Huggy Bear—*Any Starsky and Hutch fans out there?*
- iStud
- Jiggle Buns
- Kissy Muffin—*So much sugar you could get a cavity with this one.*
- Kissy Poo
- Kitty Cat—*Wonder if they ever shorten it to just "KC?"*
- Love Muffin
- Monkey Buns
- Monkey Muffins—*If you don't get the monkey love verbiage, you've never been to the zoo!*
- Moonshine
- Mr. Cutie
- Mr. Porn Muscles—*My friend's wife calls his mustache the "porn'stache."*
- PG—*Pretty sure it's short for "Pussy Galore"*
- Pooh Bear
- Pooka
- Pookie
- Pudding Pop
- Quality—*It reads well, but it sounds stilted when I say it.*
- Sailor
- Sexy Beast
- Snookums
- Snuggle Muffin
- Snugglekins
- Snugglepuff
- Snuggles—*Evidently, using any form of "snuggle" takes a potential nickname to the next level.*
- Soldier
- Squiggles—*Is Squiggles just a little sillier than Snuggles?*
- Stallion
- Sugar Lips
- Sweet Cakes
- Sweetums

- Tater Tot—*Try saying this one in a Kendrick Lamar voice.*
- Trophy
- Wiggles—*Of course, you can add silly dancing and mimic the popular children's show guys The Wiggles.*
- Zany Cat—*Why do I think there are costumes associated with this nickname?*

SEINFELD FAN FUN

CHARACTER MOST LIKELY TO BE MISTAKEN FOR SCHMOOPIE
Netta

CHARACTER MOST LIKELY TO HAVE A WARDROBE MALFUNCTION WHILE THEY'RE BEING CALLED SCHMOOPIE
Nip

CHARACTER MOST LIKELY TO CALL 900 NUMBERS AND ASK THOSE PEOPLE TO CALL THEMSELVES SCHMOOPIE
Andre (Kramer)

REAL WORLD FUN
MORE INFO

- Actress Ali Wentworth played the character of Jerry's girlfriend, Sheila, aka "Schmoopie," in "The Soup Nazi" episode of *Seinfeld*.
- Wentworth was a cast member on the Fox sketch comedy *series In Living Color*. She made correspondent appearances on *The Tonight Show With Jay Leno* and *The Oprah Winfrey Show*. Her notable film appearances include *Jerry Maguire*, *Office Space*, and *It's Complicated*. You

can see her in the sixth episode of season five of Jerry Seinfeld's *Comedians in Cars Getting Coffee*.

- Wentworth is married to George Stephanopoulos, an ABC News chief anchor correspondent and former political advisor in the Clinton Administration. They wed in 2001.
- Wentworth's mother is known as "Muffie." In fact, Muffie Cabot is an heiress and socialite who served as Nancy Reagan's social secretary in the 1980s.

FUN EXERCISE

- To help celebrate 30 years *of Seinfeld*, rank your Top 30 Schmoops. They can be from this list or complete wildcards.
- Share your list with friends, invite them to make their own lists, and have a Schmoopie Party where couples read out their lists.
- Send your best Schmoops to the Fun Stories Facebook page or Twitter page, and I'll share more of them in the future.

6

The All-You-Can-Eaters

*Y*ou might also call these people "The Kramericans." In episode after episode of *Seinfeld*, Kramer would barge into Jerry's apartment and forage for food in Jerry's refrigerator and on Jerry's shelves. This served as the inspiration for this next activity. It happens so often in the grocery store now that it won't even surprise you when I mention it.

I'm talking about people who eat or drink store items while they are shopping. Earlier, I narrated the story about The Inspiration— the water drinking, donut snarfing man I had seen in the grocery store. That happened a couple of years ago. Now, it's happening regularly.

Is everybody a Grocery Store All-You-Can-Eater now, and I missed the memo?

In an unscientific diary survey that I conducted over the course of six weeks, I saw grocery store eating happen during five of my eight visits to the store. Just like The Inspiration, these folks aren't just "visiting" the grocery store anymore—they've made themselves right at home.

Bottled water is the drink of choice. Four out of five All-You-Can-Eaters had one. I noted one incident in my diary when four ladies were talking and pushing carts, while all of them enjoyed a store brand water.

One entry with an asterisk is called "Orange Juice Guy." This guy had a full-size orange juice carton cracked open and that too, sans shopping basket. He was just sauntering down the aisle taking frequent chugs from the container. Speaking of making yourself at home, he was also wearing fuzzy slippers. I followed him for a couple of aisles to see if he'd add a food product to his experience. Sadly, or possibly thankfully, he did not. Orange Juice Guy grabbed some shampoo and headed for the checkout line. I'm betting he's in the group that doesn't make a list when he goes to the grocery store.

The grocery store often tries to get more in-store beverage activity by placing a soda machine with various sizes of plastic cups just near the front door. Now I'm thinking that is just an invitation for people to drink everything else in the store.

Now, once in a blue moon, I've grabbed a Snickers bar and given it the snuffleupagus treatment while I was shopping. I will say, however, I felt guilty about it the whole time. Then when I went to pay, I made sure I let the empty wrapper surf down the belt to the cashier. Of course, she did not greet this activity with anywhere near the enthusiasm that I received from The Superhero of Savings.

"So, it looks like you already ate this item," she said. "Snickers always satisfies," I chimed in. "Have you seen the commercials?" I added. She had not seen the commercials. She also had no idea what "hangry" means. A fun reference to Betty White's classic Snickers commercial had to be shelved for another day.

Soon, I found it hard to believe that I had once been surprised by The Inspiration's donut eating as I logged person after person eating a donut in the grocery store. And it wasn't just the glazed donuts. One person had a donut with chocolate icing that was getting all over his hands. There was no hiding the fact that he was an All-You-Can-Eater.

Thinking about my Snickers experience, I wonder how they handle the checkout after eating the donut. There's no wrapper. Do they just say, "Hey, put me down for one of those chocolate thunder donut thingies?" I'm thinking there should be a self-checkout counter right by the donuts. That would simplify the process.

Yes, it's now very easy to see people eating things while they push the cart—donuts, grapes, fruit, candy bars. It's almost as easy to see people drinking water. So far, I've only seen that one supermarket orange juice drinker, but I'm constantly on the lookout for more. I have a theory that if I break out a TV Show Jerry–inspired juice box and sip it in the store it will start a trend, but I don't want to be That Juice Guy.

Suggestion to grocery stores: Why don't you just set a flat fee, a time limit, and a designated section full of items for an all-you-can-eat (and drink) shopping experience? It would even make me consider choosing this option over going to a fast food place. Change up the items from time to time, and you'll get me in the store far more often. I'd even feel like I'm living a healthier lifestyle if I consumed more fruit because of this new section of the store. Until that time, I'm off to get some more canned pineapples.

SEINFELD FAN FUN

CHARACTER MOST LIKELY TO BE AN ALL-YOU-CAN-EATER
It's a tie between George and Newman

CHARACTER LEAST LIKELY TO BE AN ALL-YOU-CAN-EATER
Jerry

CHARACTER MOST LIKELY TO HANG OUT WITH ALL-YOU CAN-EATERS
Kramer

CHARACTER MOST LIKELY TO COMPLAIN ABOUT ALL-YOU CAN-EATERS
Estelle Costanza

CHARACTER MOST LIKELY TO BE OFFENDED BY
SMELLS EMANATING FROM ALL-YOU CAN-EATERS
Mrs. Ross

REAL WORLD FUN

MORE INFORMATION:

- Yahoo Answers reports that some people consume
  around 8,500 calories when they binge at an all-you-can-
  eat buffet.
- In an interview with NBC Sports, Michael Phelps said he
  ate approximately 12,000 calories per day during the
  2008 Summer Olympics. This included a breakfast of
  three fried egg sandwiches, a five-egg omelet, three
  pieces of French toast, three pancakes and grits. Lunch
  was typically a pound of pasta and two sandwiches.
  Later, in 2017, Phelps revised the estimate and said he
  was probably eating 8,000–10,000 calories at his peak.
- Active.com did a breakdown of what cyclists eat to ingest
  8,000 calories:

22 eggs for breakfast;
  3 cereal bars;
  14 bottles of sports drink (20 ounces each);
  4 cups of rice;
  2 cups of granola with fruit;
  8 chicken breasts; and
  4 bananas.

- Late in the summer of 2019, we reached the "too far"
  point in people eating in stores during the viral Blue Bell
  saga. At press time, at least three people had posted
  social media videos of themselves licking a carton of
  Blue Bell ice cream and then putting it back inside a

store freezer. Even though the USA Today headline —"Third ice cream licker arrested"— seems kind of funny, this was no laughing matter. I guess I have to say it: Never take a bite out of food in a grocery store—or anywhere else—and then put it back. Yes, this would have made a great *Seinfeld* topic.

FUN SEINFELD FAN EXERCISE:

Create your own *Seinfeld* character responses to the above-mentioned Blue Bell ice cream licking story.

7

The Cart Shamers

*W*here I live in Texas, and in every other place in the United States, you have the unalienable rights to life, liberty, and the pursuit of junk food in your grocery cart—you decide the order of the three. The Cart Shamers try to take all of that away.

The Cart Shamers are the people who practice the misguided art of drive-by shaming as you try to push your grocery cart past them and move happily down the aisle. They despise happiness. These nosey people like to look in your cart and make judgmental noises under their breath based on what you are purchasing that day. I sometimes call them "The Calorie Police."

There's a 1970s song by Larry Groce called "Junk Food Junkie." The song featured references to many types of junk food such as Twinkies, Fritos, and Moon Pies. It's catchy chorus closed with the words, "At night I'm a junk food junkie, good lord have pity on me." In a nutshell, you can usually find many items from the song in my grocery cart. It makes me an easy target for The Cart Shamers.

During one diary visit, I was minding my own business and scoring very high in the game where I fill my cart with many items from "Junk Food Junkie." The song mentions Ding Dongs, and I smiled because I had secured a new box of them—my wife and youngest son were hooked on to Ding Dongs at the time.

In short, our family's opinion is "Junk food is cheaper than therapy." Your family's opinions and shopping methods may differ. Consult a doctor if your grocery shopping trip lasts more than four hours.

Anyway, this holier than thou guy in a maroon, terrycloth-looking shirt starts to pass by and then stops. He shakes his head, glares at my basket, points at the Ding Dongs and says, "Oh, man. You really have zero respect for your body."

I was taken aback, but still managed to squeeze off the reply, "And you don't know the half of it. I still have dozens of items left on my list," in my best TV Show Jerry voice.

As he walked away, he said, "Make better life decisions." I almost fired back with the "jerk store" George Costanza bit from *Seinfeld*, but decided karma was already circling this Cart Shamer like a shark sensing blood in the water. And, it was almost time again for Shark Week. Who makes comments like that anyway?

Another day, I had a particular brand of spaghetti sauce in my cart along with the store brand of spaghetti noodles. This guy scopes out my cart and says in a condescending voice, "I don't mean to offend you, but there are several better brands of spaghetti sauce than that one. Also, the generic store brand of spaghetti noodles is really subpar compared to BIG NATIONAL BRAND. It's worth the extra money. Take my recommendations. You're going to thank me later."

One comment. Two criticisms. At least that's how I interpreted his "recommendations." I'm not a huge fan of the subset of The Cart Shamers, "The Recommenders."

I thanked The Recommender for his opinion, stared at his food, and decided I should just keep pushing my cart forward. I did not get the other brand of spaghetti sauce. Besides, it was full of mushrooms. I have not tried it to this day, and I probably never will. I'm also sticking with the store brand of spaghetti noodles. It's a case of The Recommender offering me a correction disguised as a recommendation. Dude made me feel like I was back in school getting called out by the teacher for a wrong answer.

If you come up against The Cart Shamer in the store, stay calm. Otherwise, you might make an oversight that could cause you to forget to buy something important on your grocery list—probably something that gets mentioned in the song "Junk Food Junkie." Forgetting an item like that puts the whole shopping trip into the family loss column when you arrive home without key items.

The Cart Shamers are sometimes disguised as The Check-Out Shamers. The Check-Out Shamers make comments while they are ringing up your items on the register. "Have you seen the calories on this one?" a Check-Out Shamer said to me one day. I had to remark that I was getting a great calories-per-dollar ratio by choosing this item. This made her think for a second and then realize I was a lost cause for her calorie crusade.

SEINFELD FAN FUN

CHARACTER MOST LIKELY TO BE A CART SHAMER WHILE WEARING A GOLDEN BOY T-SHIRT
Jerry

CHARACTER MOST LIKELY TO BE THE TARGET OF A CART SHAMER
George

CHARACTER MOST LIKELY TO RUN FROM A CART SHAMER
Kramer

CHARACTER MOST LIKELY TO TAKE CART SHAMING TO DIABOLICAL LEVELS
Crazy Joe Davola

CHARACTER MOST LIKELY TO CONFRONT A CART SHAMER
Elaine

REAL WORLD FUN

MORE INFORMATION:

- The average grocery store cart weighs 70 pounds.
- Grocery carts cost anywhere from $100 to $150 apiece with metal ones costing more and those with more plastic costing less.
- The online site carts4u.com sells the Standard Grocery Shopping Cart for $148 each. If you buy 50 of them, you can get a discount price of just $130 each.
- The Food Marketing Institute reports that nearly 2 million shopping carts are stolen each year—and that's only in the food industry.
- The song "Junk Food Junkie" by Larry Groce reached #9 on the Billboard Hot 100 in 1976.
- The song was performed by Mackenzie Phillips and The Jacksons on the June 23, 1976 episode of *The Jacksons* TV variety show.

8

The Egg Swappers

*T*here's a lot of information about eggs in my diary. You're probably familiar with this next activity. Yes, I've done this one. It starts with you opening an egg crate to check for broken eggs. When you see one (or more), you open another egg carton and swap an unbroken one for any broken ones you find. I call these people The Egg Swappers.

One day, I saw a guy who had three different cartons open. He spent a couple of minutes carefully holding each one up and switching out the broken ones. I usually do my switching very quickly. How do you do it?

I don't know how stores feel about The Egg Swappers, but I feel like it is a reasonably OK practice so long as you switch out broken ones for the same size unbroken eggs. But I watched one guy switching out three unbroken large eggs for three unbroken jumbo eggs. To me, that's over the line. Who does that? Is it some kind of silly game where he puts more and more jumbo ones in the large carton each time? Is it a money-saving measure? He's probably a millionaire, and this is how he gets his kicks.

For many years, the most broken eggs I had personally encountered when I opened a carton was four. There were two together in that batch, and then one on each side. During the diary survey period, however, the record was smashed—literally. I opened up a carton to find egg soup. All 12 eggs were broken! I'm thinking someone dropped the carton and then slipped it back into the middle of the stack of cartons. Seeing all 12 eggs swimming in a yolk lake was new territory—those crazy Egg Swappers!

One person I observed needs to be mentioned here as well. Dude went next level with egg swapping. He pulled an item out of his pocket that looked like a pen. He started holding the eggs up, turning them around and clicking the pen, which was actually a very bright little flashlight. I'm guessing he was looking for double yolks.

Watching him took me back to a story my dad had told me a long time ago; it was about how he used to earn some extra money when he was young by helping a friend's family "candle" the eggs at their local farm. The UK's Daily Express says "candling" eggs involves holding the egg up to the light and seeing through the shell. They say if you hold a 100-watt bulb in a small box with a hole in it, which is slightly smaller than the egg, and then place the egg over the hole, you can see the yolks. Egg distributors evidently do this regularly, which is how boxes of double-yolk eggs can be offered.

According to an article by Dr. Karl Kruszelnicki, when you average out the number of double-yolk eggs from chickens of all ages, about one out of every 1,000 eggs has two yolks. He goes on to say that double yolks happen more frequently in chickens aged 20–28 weeks old. These young chickens produce a double yolk once every 100 times they lay an egg. I'm thinking my special pen guy in the store must really love eggs if the chances of a double yolk are just 1 in 1,000.

Wideopenpets.com says eggs from chickens with access to green plants and insects look a lot different than those from factory-raised chickens that never go outdoors. Furthermore, they say a deep orange yolk means the egg is from pasture-raised hens and indicates the chicken had a well-balanced and healthy diet and that the egg itself has excellent nutritional value. Can my guy see any of this with his pen light? Does he have his own egg detection superpowers?

Onehundreddollarsamonth.com says if your recipe calls for egg yolks only, you need to pay attention to the yolk size. Sometimes your double yolkers will have half-size yolks, so two would count as one. But if they are full-size, you'd count them as two separate yolks. For full eggs in a recipe, just go by weight.

Eggsafety.org says an egg with a double yolk is said to bring good luck when you find it. Maybe my pen light guy is looking for luck.

TRIPLE YOLK

The British Egg Information Service says the odds of getting a triple-yolk egg are one in 25 million.

WORLD RECORD

According to the Guinness World Records, the most yolks found in one chicken egg was 9. I'm thinking they used some kind of super special light to properly identify all nine of those yolks. You might even need an independent accounting firm if you get assigned to that project.

THE UNBELIEVABLE EGG DAY

During the survey period, I had a most remarkable egg experience that may never again happen in my lifetime. It was some kind of great egg karma winking at me and thanking me for showing eggs some love in this book. I was making a version of scrambled eggs that we call "Hippo" at my house. Without divulging our secret recipe, I can tell you it starts with ham and shredded cheese. I was making a batch for our whole crew, so 12 eggs needed to be cracked.

I shook my head approvingly when the first egg I cracked was a double yolk. When I cracked the second egg, it was also a double yolk. I had done that before a few times in my life, but not in many years. Are you ready for this? When I cracked number three, it was also a double yolk! I had never had three-in-a-row, or even three double yolks in a dozen.

I held my breath and cracked number four. Yes! It was also a double yolker! The streak ended at four, as the fifth one was normal. I was still chattering about it when I reached egg number 11, and it was also a double yolk! There were five double yolks in the carton. Egg number 12 was not a double yolk. Still, five double yolks in a carton of eggs! Like a rarely seen comet, this was probably a once-in-a-lifetime occurrence. Yep, it's the little things that make life so special!

If you want to have some fun, read this story with somebody that you regularly cook with—your spouse/significant other/child. Discuss it and then let a couple of weeks pass. Find a store that sells cartons of double yolk eggs. Slip lots of them into a regular carton of eggs. Sometime later, ask this person to help you make some eggs. Use your camera phone and watch them freak out when the double yolks just keep coming. Post the results on any of the Fun Stories sites.

SUGGESTED SEINFELD-RELATED FAN TERMS

- The Double Yolkers
- The Sunny Siders

SEINFELD FAN FUN

CHARACTER MOST LIKELY TO BE AN EGG SWAPPER
George

CHARACTER LEAST LIKELY TO BE AN EGG SWAPPER
Jerry

CHARACTER MOST LIKELY TO BE ANNOYED BY EGG
SWAPPERS WHO SWAP DIFFERENT SIZES OF EGGS
George

CHARACTER MOST LIKELY TO DATE AN EGG SWAPPER
WHILE WEARING A STAINED RED SHIRT
George

CHARACTERS MOST LIKELY TO FORM A STRANGE BUT
FUNNY EGG-SWAPPING ALLIANCE
Elaine and Frank Costanza

TRUE OR FALSE: RUTHIE COHEN WAS AN EGG
SWAPPER.
True. You can't work in a diner for that many episodes and not have
some type of egg swapping situations.

REAL WORLD FUN

MORE INFORMATION

- According to the Washington Post, Americans are eating
  eggs in numbers not seen in more than 50 years.
  Americans eat about 279 eggs per year, per person,
  which averages out to about 95 million dozen eggs
  nationwide.
- Backyard Chickens reports that we eat 1.3 tons of eggs,
  or 19,826 individual eggs, in a lifetime.
- World Atlas says Japan consumes more eggs than
  anywhere else in the world. People in Japan eat an
  average of 320 eggs annually.
- Paraguay is second with an average of 309 eggs
  annually.
- China is third with an average of 300 eggs per year.
- The United States is not in the top 10.

- Here are positions 4–10:

(4) Mexico
(5) Ukraine
(6) Malaysia
(7) Brunei
(8) Slovakia
(9) Belarus
(10) The Russian Federation

Confession: I didn't have any knowledge of the Nation of Brunei, the Abode of Peace, before I conducted a little egg research. It sounds like a great Kramer conversation starter to me.

The American Idols

*S*eeing people spontaneously break into song in the grocery store is almost as much fun as watching Elaine dance badly in "The Little Kicks" episode of *Seinfeld* (Season 8, Episode 4). I'm especially drawn to anybody who sings with extra passion, as if they might be auditioning for *American Idol*. I like to imagine they have been waiting outside the grocery store for 10 hours, and this is their moment to try and get a golden ticket to Hollywood. That's why I call them The American Idols in my diary entries.

Some sing just to be singing. Others are performing while they shop. They're singing the words to the Muzak and doing little dances and hand gestures as they smile at you. They're hoping you work for a major record label, and/or you are a talent scout. I once said to one of them in my best Seacrest voice, "This is American Idol!" That mildly amused the lady.

Try to have fun with this phenomenon if you see it in your grocery store. You'd ruin their day if you went all Randy Jackson on them and said, "Your singing was just alright, it was a little pitchy, dog."

The most notable thing I've seen in relation to this activity happened one Saturday morning at around 10 am. I was grabbing some eggs and had assembled a perfect dozen in the jumbo size. I was sans flashlight, but the carton was now sans cracks and broken shells. The opening piano notes of the song "I Will Survive" by Gloria Gaynor came across the store speakers. The woman just down the aisle from me looked like she had walked right out of an episode of "Glee." Suddenly, she had transformed from quiet and reserved to donut display diva pumping her hands and belting out, "First I was afraid, I was petrified…"

As I turned the corner with my basket, I picked up the whispery strains of another woman singing, "… kept thinking I could never live without you by my side…" This was such a rush for me that I quickly raced my cart to try and find another singer in the next aisle.

I struck out in that aisle, but two aisles later, I picked up another person singing near the popcorn, "Not I, I will survive…" Greedy now, after having achieved a Gloria Gaynor Hat Trick (three people), I turned into Speed Racer and raced the cart across the store to what I thought was a sure bet—the makeup aisle.

When I hit the makeup aisle, I heard singing. Yes, it was happening! The person had long hair. Then *he* flipped around as he sang "I Will Survive." That was extra fun for me, baby! (Say that last sentence in a George Costanza voice.) Put it on the scoreboard. I had successfully found four people singing the same song in the store!

I really think I could have found a fifth singer that day, but I felt like I needed to leave it right there in case I ever heard the song again in this store—or another store. It's sometimes fun to leave the record within reach.

I made a diary entry alongside this activity. Two songs came to mind that I think might stand a chance at challenging the "I Will Survive" record of four singers.

"We Will Rock You" by Queen gets a lot of people singing. It's a sports anthem and is more popular now because of the recent *Bohemian Rhapsody* movie. How many store singers could it get?

I'm also thinking "Don't Stop Believin'" by Journey might be able to hit double digits. Whenever I've played this song over the speakers at our high school baseball stadium, it has turned into a crowd sing-along. "Just a small town girl, living in a lonely world. She took the midnight train going…" You probably said "anywhere" as you finished the last line. I've even had fans say "Awwwww" when I stopped the song because the inning was about to start.

Do you control the music for a grocery store? Please try this and report the results back to us. I would love to see some video of that test as well!

Team Taylor Swift, I'm not trying to tell you your business, but it seems like there is a lot of extra opportunity to promote songs in grocery stores. And I'd much rather go home singing a Taylor Swift song than most of the tunes I hear in the grocery store.

Bottom line is you need an anthem if you are going to get groups of people to sing the same song in the grocery store. Maybe your group could plan a flash mob for a slow day at the grocery store. The possibilities are endless…

This has been The American Idols. Seacrest, out. (SOUND OF ME DROPPING THE MIC)

SEINFELD FAN FUN

MOST LIKELY TO SING IN THE STORE
Elaine

MOST LIKELY TO SHUSH PEOPLE IF THEY TALK WHILE "DESPERADO" IS PLAYING IN THE STORE
Brett

LEAST LIKELY TO SING IN THE STORE UNLESS A GIRL IS INVOLVED AND THEN HE'LL DO IT QUICKLY AND WITH A LOT OF SNARK
Jerry

MOST LIKELY TO TRY AND MANAGE THE CAREER OF A

PERSON THEY SEE SINGING IN THE STORE
Kramer

MOST LIKELY TO TRY AND GET AN UNADVERTISED
DISCOUNT RELATED TO STORE SINGING
George

COMPANY MOST LIKELY TO PAY TOO MUCH TO TRY
AND SPONSOR A SINGER THEY SEE IN THE GROCERY
STORE
Kruger Industrial Smoothing

REAL WORLD FUN

BONUS INFORMATION

- Speaking of singing in a public place, the next time you are on YouTube, check out the 1985 McDonald's McD.L.T. (remember that one?) commercial featuring the happy clapping and dancing song stylings of Jason Alexander!
- Today reports that for "American Idol 4," 21,000 people showed up to audition in Washington, D.C.
- Can you name Ryan Seacrest's co-host in the first season of *American Idol*? The answer is Brian Dunkleman.
- Stars such as Lady Antebellum's Hillary Scott and songstress Colbie Caillet were both rejected during *American Idol* auditions.
- Entertainment Weekly reports that Paula Abdul quit during her first day on the job—8 times—but she then stayed and remained a judge for eight seasons.
- Do you remember that Ellen DeGeneres was a judge on *American Idol* during season nine?

10

The No Cart Mozarts

*O*f course, Bruce Springsteen gave us the lyric "Go Cart Mozart" in his 1973 song "Blinded By The Light" from his debut album "Greetings From Asbury Park, N.J." Manfred Mann's Earth Band covered the song in 1976 and hit #1. There's even an English indie pop band named Go-Kart Mozart.

If you see through Seinfeld Eyes, however, then the No Cart Mozarts are people who refuse to use grocery carts. They stuff their arms full of items on their grocery list and consider themselves ahead of the game for not having to drag around a clunky cart.

"No, I don't need a cart. I'm good," said one of these No Cart Mozarts recently when I was at the store. An attentive store employee had pushed a cart his way since he had been waddling around the store with overflowing arms. I was wondering if we could put a frozen pizza box on his head and test whether he could balance it all the way to the register. If not, I was willing to time how long he could balance it before it fell.

The No Cart Mozarts start off thinking they are saving a lot of time and effort with their grocery store approach. Many times, however, they end up putting things back so that another, more important item will fit into their arms. That's a time-consuming process that needs much careful consideration.

Once, a No Cart Mozart with his arms full asked me to hand him a six-pack of beer. I tried to hand him cans, and he was flabbergasted at my choice. He wanted the bottles. I later noted "wanted bottles" and underlined it in my diary. Then, No Cart asked me to hold on while he re-positioned some items in his arms. Finally, he asked me what he should put back to make room for the beer. I was thinking he should drop it all—into a grocery cart. Besides, that would let him upgrade from a six-pack to a 12-pack of beer.

ME: You are quite the No Cart Mozart

DUDE: Come again?

ME: You know—no basket. You're a No Cart Mozart.

DUDE: No thanks. I'm good. I don't need a cart.

ME: Have a great day, Mozart!

DUDE: Carts have a lot of germs.

SEINFELD FAN FUN

CHARACTER MOST LIKELY TO BE A NO CART MOZART
Kramer

CHARACTER LEAST LIKELY TO BE A NO CART MOZART

George

CHARACTER MOST LIKELY TO DATE A NO CART
MOZART WHEN SHE'S OUT THERE
Estelle Costanza

CHARACTER MOST LIKELY TO COMPLAIN ABOUT A
NO CART MOZART
Helen Seinfeld

CHARACTER MOST LIKELY TO CONFRONT A NO CART
MOZART
Frank Costanza

REAL WORLD FUN

BONUS INFORMATION

Despite being one of the most successful musicians in the history of the world, Bruce Springsteen has never had a solo #1 song on the Billboard Hot 100. He had one as part of the USA For Africa with the charity single "We Are The World." He also achieved a #1 as the writer of "Blinded By The Light" when Manfred Mann's Earth Band took the song to #1.

Let that be a boost to your self-esteem the next time you think you're not getting enough credit for something at work or home. One of the most successful musicians of all time does not have a solo #1 on the Hot 100—I'm sure Bruce doesn't lose any sleep over pop music charts.

The Dr. Feelgoods

*N*o Cart Mozart's commentary about cart germs stuck with me. Even though he was pretty wacky, I got this vibe that he knew what he was talking about. It made me watch out for the germ brigade with my Seinfeld Eyes.

I saw all sorts of things that I noted in my diary. It made me wonder how all of this grocery store germ-fighting activity had previously escaped my radar. Now that I knew about it, I started seeing it everywhere. I saw people wearing masks in the store and/or going crazy with hand sanitizer. Cleansing wipes came up everywhere. Seeing the masks made me think of doctors, which then made me think not about the medical profession, but about Mötley Crüe's classic rock song "Dr. Feelgood."

The random thoughts don't stop there.

Seeing any type of hand sanitizer or sanitizing wipes often makes me think of the *Seinfeld* episode "The Bubble Boy." (Season 4, Episode 7) You probably know the episode. In short, a boy had to live in a plastic bubble due to immune deficiencies. You just knew, because it was *Seinfeld*, that something was going to happen that would pop the bubble. And it did. It doesn't seem like a laugh-worthy topic. In true *Seinfeld* fashion, however, George gets into an argument with the boy, and the bubble gets broken. It's one of those preposterous episodes that some thought crossed the line.

Speaking of preposterous, I've gained a new appreciation for the sanitary wipes available very close to the storage bins where I get a cart at a couple of different grocery stores. I saw an online Reader's Digest article that said shopping carts are some of the absolute dirtiest of public surfaces. The article cited a University of Arizona research study where researches sampled 85 grocery store shopping carts in various West Coast cities. What did they find? They found that cart surfaces had exponentially more bacteria than what they had measured in over 100 public restrooms, which included toilet seats and flush handles. In fact, 50% of the 85 shopping carts were found to carry E. coli. No Cart Mozart is suddenly smarter than I previously thought, plus he buys good beer.

During the diary period, I saw this lady pull out one of these sanitary wipes and practically take a shower.

Then it happened.

Right out of the list of suggestions from the Reader's Digest article, this germophobe pulled out her own snap-on. I know some of you are thinking I said "strap-on." You get points for imagination, but I'm saying she had her own sanitary snap-on cart handle that she put on the cart to help keep it germ-free.

I was impressed. When I looked online, I found a 16" vibrant red shopping cart handle cover with a healthy hands logo. The ad said that it is easy to slip on and has a washable vinyl surface. This item cost $8.99, but there were suggestions for similar deluxe items that cost $10.99. Please, Larry David, work this item into an episode of *Curb Your Enthusiasm*!

Finally, I didn't see one during my unscientific study, but the article suggested that protective seat covers might be used to minimize germs for kids as they sit in the carts. Soon, we'll need to carry large bags to the store that are full of all of our sanitary supplies. If we do that, they'll tell us how unsanitary the outer surface of these bags is. If you are a wicked smart scientist, can't you just make us a store with a bubble over it?

Watch out for the Moops.

. . .

SEINFELD FAN FUN

CHARACTER MOST LIKELY TO BE A DR. FEELGOOD
Jerry

CHARACTER LEAST LIKELY TO BE A DR. FEELGOOD
Poppie

CHARACTER MOST LIKELY TO USE INFORMATION
FROM THIS STORY TO TRY AND GET EXTRA TIME OFF
FROM WORK
George

CHARACTER MOST LIKELY TO USE A CART SNAP-ON
Kramer

CHARACTER MOST LIKELY TO MAKE BAD JOKES
ABOUT DR. FEELGOODS AND CART SNAP-ONS
Kenny Bania

CHARACTER MOST LIKELY TO CATCH YOU PICKING
YOUR NOSE IN THE STORE
Tia Van Camp

REAL WORLD FUN

MORE INFORMATION

- The person who played Mel Sanger, the Yoo-hoo
  delivery truck driver and father of the Bubble Boy in

"The Bubble Boy" episode of Seinfeld, is Brian Doyle-Murray. He's the older brother of actor Bill Murray. Doyle is his grandmother's maiden name. He chose to hyphenate it to avoid confusion with another actor. Brian Doyle-Murray ended up appearing in three different *Seinfeld* episodes. He was also in "The Pilot, Part Two," and "The Finale, Part 2."

- A University of Arizona study ranked shopping carts third on the list of nastiest public items to touch, with only playground equipment and the armrests on public transportation producing more germ-laden results.
- The New Hampshire Public Radio compiled a list of five of the most successful germaphobes:

Howard Hughes—The famous billionaire is probably the most widely publicized germaphobe.

Howard Stern—Does the name "Howard" have a special connection to germaphobia? The King of All Media is a self-professed homebody and germaphobe who feels uncomfortable with live appearances.

Howie Mandel—There's that "Howard" link again. Mandel once said, "In my mind, my hand is like a petri dish."

Donald Trump—It makes it quite interesting that Trump, a germophobe, is President of the United States, but doesn't enjoy shaking hands.

Nikola Tesla—According to Mental Floss, Tesla was a germaphobe to the point that he used 17 clean towels a day and had a violent aversion against the earrings of women.

• "Dr. Feelgood" is the fifth studio album released by heavy metal band Mötley Crüe in 1989. It is the band's best-selling album, plus its only album to top the Billboard 200 chart.

12

The Shelf Climbers

*T*his next diary entry can get pretty wacky—and pretty dangerous. Observe it through your Seinfeld Eyes, but steer clear of performing it with your actual limbs. Thankfully, I've never witnessed anybody getting hurt doing it. I'm talking about the people who need something from the very top shelf in a grocery store. They can't reach it, so they devise several different strategies to get the item. My favorite one is climbing. I call these people "The Shelf Climbers."

On many occasions, I see people struggling in various mountain climbing positions as they try to reach things on the highest shelves. Many times, they've used the lower shelves as a convenient ladder in pursuit of their prized item.

Some people need help because they start to climb and then just get stuck there like a cat in a tree. It may be that they are too scared to continue, or worried that the shelf they are using as a ladder is about to give out and send them crashing to the ground.

Other people in this category are "The Jumpers." They think if they just start jumping, their body will turn into a pogo stick, and they'll magically reach the item they need. No matter what type of shoes this person is wearing, it amuses me to nickname these people "Air Jordan." It's probably because Michael Jordan was one of the best jumpers of all time, and some of these folks can barely jump a couple of inches, yet they somehow think they can get to their desired item and grab it. It's air-headed thinking, to say the least.

A third group within this realm is "The Yellers." Once I saw a guy who needed a special type of crackers, and they were way up there on the sky shelf (top shelf). Dude just starts yelling, "Hey, who put the damn crackers so high on the shelf? I need some crackers right now! Who's doing this? I need some damn crackers!"

In his mind, store employees were going to hear his yelling, drop everything, and run like superheroes to help him.

That didn't happen.

I got tired of hearing him yell, so I reached up and got the crackers. He was mid yell when I handed him the packet and kept walking. Nevertheless, he still needed to yell one more time to properly quench his rage. In his defense, his strategy had worked. He had gotten his crackers. It bothered me a little bit that I had enabled him. It also bothered me that Mr. Yeller had not said thank you.

Full disclosure, I am not usually a shelf helper, or even a store helper. My wife, Jenny, however, is a first-ballot hall-of-fame grocery store helper. Jenny is pretty tall, so she's naturally suited to be a shelf helper.

It's quite surprising how many times we have found someone staring at an item on the top shelf. She seems to be a magnet for this type of thing. Her helping radar goes off, and she automatically asks them if she can help. In almost all the cases, she gets them their item and makes a new friend along the way.

People are very grateful when you get an item down from the top shelf for them. I think this is because they place a disproportionate value on the item once it appears that they will not be able to acquire it. Then, Superhero Jenny swoops in and saves the day!

I usually like to tell Jenny, "Another successful day of saving the universe. Tell Superman and Batman hello," when she finishes one of these missions.

I'm seriously considering writing a children's book called "Jenny the Shelf Helper." I should, but I can't resist telling you to look for the book in the "Shelf Help" section.

On a final note, it's especially funny to watch people move in and out of the different phases we've mentioned in this story. A person might first be a Yeller. In a minute or two, they might progress to being a Jumper. If that doesn't help, they turn into a Shelf Climber. I could sometimes kick myself for stepping in to help the yelling guy before I could properly observe whether he would progress to jumping and/or shelf climbing. I think I had a mild headache, and his yelling was making it worse.

SEINFELD FAN FUN

MOST LIKELY TO USE SPECIAL SHOES TO BE A SHELF CLIMBER
Jimmy

MOST LIKELY TO HELP A SHELF CLIMBER
Kramer

MOST LIKELY TO COMMENT ABOUT A SHELF CLIMBER
Jerry

MOST LIKELY TO TRY AND GET AN UNEXPECTED DISCOUNT RELATED TO SHELF CLIMBING
George

WHO'S MOST LIKELY TO BE A SHELF CLIMBER: LARRY DAVID, OR LARRY DAVID'S GEORGE STEINBRENNER CHARACTER?
Larry David's George Steinbrenner character

REAL WORLD FUN

. . .

Bonus First-Person Shelf Climbing/Jumping Incident

My youngest son, Griffin, is now 6'2" tall. His height comes in handy. It can also be dangerous.

Last week, we were grocery shopping in the big Super Store. He wanted Cheetos Puffs. He spotted them on the shelf, searched for the biggest bag, and threw one in the cart.

For those of you keeping score at home, the male-bonding commentary I used for this activity was, "LeBron, searching for snacks, finds the cheesy bag. LeBron grabs the bag, spins away from double coverage, and dunks it! Folks, that's a SportsCenter Top Ten Play of the Day!"

Just as we were celebrating another grocery store victory, Griff spotted a much larger bag of Cheetos Puffs that seemed to be nesting in its own world above the clouds. It was on a shelf so high that I hadn't even seen it during my normal grocery store browsing. I called it "Mount Cheetos."

The game was on.

Could Griff get it?

For grocery store basketball players like us, there was a blue strip along the top shelf that said, "Ask for assistance." This could have meant lots of things. It's a gray area. It most certainly did not say, "Don't jump like LeBron trying to get the biggest bag of Cheetos Puffs that we are actually trying to sell to tall customers just like you."

Disclaimer: If you see this blue strip, please make the safest decision. Do not ask yourself, "What would LeBron do?"

Now that we have that out of the way, of course Griff had to score the biggest bag. That shelf would have been empty if they hadn't wanted anyone interacting with it.

Griff realized the degree of difficulty was abnormally high since he hadn't worn his basketball shoes and instead had some cheap plastic sandals on. Kids his age call them Jandals (Jesus Sandals). I hope that this is a respectful reference and not something I shouldn't have shared here. Anyway, I started to get worried. I've never seen LeBron do any dunking in plastic sandals that are usually reserved as throw-on shoes for quick store trips, or chores your parents have been asking you to do for so long that you really just need to get it over with.

Griff did a cursory jump in the Jandals and didn't like the push-off or the landing. He kicked them off. He was going to use the all-socks method. Griff got pretty high, but could only touch the bottom of the first bag on Mount Cheetos. This was going to require a Lebron-style running start!

A teenage couple came walking down the aisle as Griff paced it off. I asked them if they wanted to see something they might be talking about for the rest of the year. They seemed confused and said "Okay." I told them Griff was an extra in the last Cheetos commercial, and he was re-enacting something he had done on the Internet a few months ago. It was enough to get some of their divided attention.

Then, Griff said "Lebron Mode" and bounded toward the shelf. The top of his hand reached Mount Cheetos and successfully brought down a large bag. I was Triple Dad Proud—that's roughly the equivalent of successfully making good on a triple dog dare.

I clapped—I love to clap in the store when getting groceries—and told the people they had been especially lucky to witness such a feat. They seemed to have thought it was fun and offered Griff a quick "Congratulations, man." Griff just wanted to get to the next aisle so that he could get his grocery store experience–lovin' dad out of there.

13

The Grinch Checkers

*T*he cash register workers at a store where I shop are trained to go out of their way to greet customers as they start ringing up their items. It's almost embarrassing how friendly and upbeat some of them are. They ask me about my day and whether I found everything I needed, among other select niceties. Sometimes it almost makes me blush. I actually feel like they care about me as a person. In my mind, I have a giddy reaction similar to Elaine's on *Seinfeld* when things are really going her way.

The other day, however, my turn came, and the cash register person didn't speak. It was jarring. There was no smile, no glowing compliments about my shopping prowess—nothing. I'm talking complete radio silence. In fact, she barely looked up as she speed checked my items. I must mention that she was very fast at ringing them up. It didn't even phase me when she threw a couple of cans on top of the bread and the Doritos. Soon, all of the items were rung up, and she used some more of her Jedi mind tricks to get me to quickly put my credit card into the machine and pay.

The receipt came out and she handed it to me—all the while staring at my orange cloth bags that were lying in the middle of the items I had purchased. She was officially finished with my transaction. The only bagging she was going to do was the bagging of her responsibility of bagging my items.

I was in a good mood, so I played the game and bagged my things. Sometimes, I pride myself in being the trusted helper by bagging my own things when I see the store is smashed, and the checker has a long line. On this day, however, there was nobody behind me. She was just being lazy—and quiet as a mouse.

At one point, I slowed down the pace of my bagging to see if she would join in to make the rest of the process go faster. When I looked up, she was on her phone. She was still so finished with me. There was not even going to be a "thank you." I usually received at least two or three cheerful "thank yous" at this store.

I looked around. I thought I was surely on a reality prank show with hidden cameras. Or, perhaps they were shooting a grocery store instructional video where she was serving as the "before" person who would later be intercut with the friendlier "after" person who helps everybody. To the best of my knowledge, that sort of thing was not happening.

I decided to make it official. She was a Grinch Checker. Max the dog and the newer Yak sidekick were missing, or we could have started a Grinch movie reboot right on the spot. All of the Whos in Whoville could have fit nicely into this situation. I waved goodbye to her and offered my fake TV Show Jerry smile. The Grinch just gave me an unfriendly blink.

I never saw The Grinch Checker again in that store. I'm guessing she lasted another couple of hours before somebody went Newman (aka postal) on her. I later searched on Google, YouTube, Facebook, and Instagram for "Silent Checkout Prank" but found nothing.

During the whole drive home, I tried to come up with possible reasons for her behavior. I also thought about Whoville and hearts that grow multiple sizes. I thought about the true meaning of no hugging, no learning. Of all the crazy things I contemplated about The Grinch Checker's behavior, these were my five finalists…

- #1: She's a newly minted member of the witness protection program, and the store is employing her at the government's request. Project Silent Shopper is an important part of our national security efforts. I inadvertently did my country a great service by not complaining, bagging my own groceries, and helping her assimilate. I may even receive a medal later in the program.

- #2: She's a low-talker, and I just didn't hear all of the things she was saying to me. I'm just thankful I do not own a pirate shirt, or a puffy shirt. Say it with me, "I don't want to be a pirate!"

- #3: Grinchie's boyfriend and BFFs were secretly watching her on Facetime and getting a huge chuckle at her "Silent Susie" routine. My confused face was made into dozens of memes that are still very popular in many parts of the US and Canada.

- #4: Grinchie bet all of her store friends that she could do an entire customer check-out without speaking. After I left, she collected hundreds of dollars in winnings, bought a Powerball ticket, won $250 million, and is now retired and living in Florida at Del Boca Vista phase III.

- #5: Grinchie knows I'm on the fringe of the author game, am writing a book with a *Seinfeld Eyes* grocery theme, and she wanted to make sure she got included in one of the stories. The odds of this scenario being correct are about the equivalent of Kramer making good on that oil tanker rubber bladder idea.

SEINFELD FAN FUN

CHARACTER THAT COULD BECOME A GRINCH
CHECKER THE FASTEST
Jack Klompus

CHARACTER MOST LIKELY TO EXPERIENCE A GRINCH
CHECKER
Jerry

CHARACTER LEAST LIKELY TO EXPERIENCE A GRINCH
CHECKER
Elaine

CHARACTER CAPABLE OF MAKING THE CRAZIEST
GRINCH FACE
Elaine

CHARACTER MOST LIKELY TO BE CALLED A GRINCH
George

CHARACTER MOST LIKELY TO MAKE FRIENDS WITH A
GRINCH CHECKER
Kramer

REAL WORLD FUN

MORE INFORMATION

- The Grinch is a fictional character created by Dr. Seuss. The book *How the Grinch Stole Christmas* first appeared in 1957.
- The Grinch first appeared in the May 1955 issue of Redbook in a 32-line poem called "The Hoobub and the Grinch."
- In 1966, the story was adapted into an animated TV feature. Boris Karloff served as both the story's narrator and the voice of the Grinch.
- Many people incorrectly think Karloff also sang the song, "You're A Mean One, Mr. Grinch," but Karloff

couldn't sing. Thurl Ravenscroft sang the song. That's great trivia for your next holiday Happy Hour.

- The Grinch has been played/voiced by many different actors including Boris Karloff, Hans Conried, Bob Holt, Anthony Asbury, Jim Carrey, and Benedict Cumberbatch.

14

The Bread Hulks

*H*oly, marble rye! ("The Rye," Season 7, Episode 11). Needless to say, I learned a lot about bread as this next story unfolded.

According to Quora, 99.8% of people eat bread. In fact, each person in the United States consumes an average of 60.3 loaves a year. For 2017, that meant 19.6 billion loaves of bread. It also means 8.8 million loaves of bread are baked in a day. According to nationalfestivalofbreads.com, Kansas is the largest wheat producing state. Nearly one-fifth of all wheat grown in the United States is grown in Kansas, which has about 20,000 wheat farmers. All the wheat grown in Kansas in a single year would fit in a train stretching from western Kansas to the Atlantic Ocean.

This bread fascination took shape when I started recognizing that more than other items in the store, people like to interact with the bread as they decide whether to buy it. This usually involves squeezing it—usually in a not-so-gentle manner.

Side note, if you're already thinking about it, the "man hands" episode of *Seinfeld* is called "The Bizarro Jerry" (Season 8, Episode 3).

Anyway, I started calling these not-so-gentle bread squeezers "Bread Hulks." My sons had these fake, big green Hulk hands when they were young. The hands even had Hulk sound effects. They were very popular Christmas presents. I wish we still had them. I would have brought them to the store and gotten a few pictures of me wearing them as I manhandle some bread.

We've all been there. It's Sunday night, and we decide we need to make a store run or the Monday versions of ourselves will be very unhappy that there is no bread to make a sandwich for lunch. The grocery store looks quite different on Sunday night. The lighting feels a little darker and hazy. It's like the aftermath of a big rock concert, when all the fireworks have gone off, and the music is only a memory. On Sunday nights at the grocery store, there's more trash, less camaraderie, and everything is picked over—especially the bread.

When there's only a loaf or two of bread left, there is about a 90% chance that they've been handled by Hulks. I consider it a good day if 75% of the pieces pass my visual inspection of whether they have been Hulk-squashed. For whatever reason, even if there are only two loaves of bread left in the whole store, I still inspect them. In my mind, it's like the world is coming to an end, and we only have room for one loaf of bread in our emergency supplies—so we must choose wisely. The fate of at least five upcoming lunches depends on this moment.

I've pondered opening the two loaves of bread, removing the smashed pieces, and making one perfectly good loaf of bread. But then, I've also decided that even though people are eating and drinking things all over the store, swapping out eggs, and climbing into the milk cooler, we have still not reached the day where it is acceptable to open loaves of bread and swap out the smashed pieces for good ones.

I sometimes see the Bread Hulks squeeze bread, then smell it. It's very primal. One guy stood there, hands locked in the squeeze, and smelled the bread for about 15 seconds. Is this related to peach smelling? I've never seen anything like it outside of wine tasters.

Long story short, after all of that, he put it back. Clearly, the loaf had not met his Hulk standards.

The same Bread Hulk then squeezed another loaf, and smelled it again. He put this second one back—and then grabbed the one underneath it and put it in his cart. The chosen one had not been squeezed or smelled. I don't know why. I guess two loaves needed Hulk testing before the third one finally got the Bread Hulk Seal of Approval.

I'd like to admit that one of the Bread Hulks recently taught me an economics lesson that temporarily turned my world upside down. It involves bread size. Since my oldest guy went to college, our bread consumption has gone down. My wife is a CPA. She is very good at auditing our expenses. We decided to save money by buying the smaller loaf. That also means we would waste less bread.

This was going well for many months until I saw this Bread Hulk squeeze test the small-sized loaf and then the large-sized loaf. Then he looked closely at both of them and chose the larger loaf. It seemed like a case of this Bread Hulk needing more toast and sand-wiches. The way he stared down the loaves seemed far from pedes-trian Bread Hulk activity. It made me curious, so I had to take a look as well.

Upon further review, and maybe this happens at your store, I saw that the smaller loaf actually costs a little more than the larger one. It was 11 cents on this particular day. How does that math work? I guess the good folks in Kansas think that if you are going to buy less of a product, you need to pay more. What's next? Six eggs for a higher price than 12 eggs?

These Bread Hulks had gotten in my head.

Depression set in. The small bread, higher price dilemma was the reverse of my milk upgrade fun. I'd downgraded myself (and my entire family) with every small loaf purchase. Every consumer that buys the large loaf is not only getting more bread than me, they are also getting a better price. I visualized a long line of shoppers each purchasing a large bread as they mocked me and said, "11 cents! 11 cents! 11 cents!" My mind multiplied 11 cents by 52 weeks a year, and then by 10 years. I wondered how much that lost money could have accumulated in the stock market.

My mind needed an idea to quiet down this bread math storm. I decided, for a little while, that the smaller loaf had better taste, got squashed less, and was basically the equivalent of top-shelf liquor. Those thoughts temporarily settled my mind, but I knew it wouldn't last.

What followed was a cost-per-piece analysis situation at my house. Grilled cheese sandwiches were discussed. Gas prices were discussed. Calculators were heavily used, but none were harmed in the making of the final decision on bread size.

We ended up choosing the...(*drumroll please*)

Small bread. What was the deciding factor? This somewhat scientific process of decision making led to my wife saying we were going to stay with the smaller size. It felt right. My inner spin doctor reviewed the process and stamped it as a win for everybody. The store gets more money. The farmers get more money. There is less wasted bread. Our family eats a little less bread, and that's good for our waistline.

I hear you saying, in your Costanza voice, "But what about the 11 extra cents, Scott?" And what happens next is a classic example of what can happen when you see the grocery store (and math, and the whole universe) through Seinfeld Eyes. I call it The Golden Opportunity.

Rather than feeling like everybody else who buys the large bread is getting 11 cents ahead of me, I've convinced myself that I have struck a deal with the universe that officially counter-balances any guilt associated with one of my other frequent grocery store activities. Yep, I'm now guilt-free about any wasted milk that expires because of my Plus 3, Plus 4, and Plus 5 shopping trips.

That is 11 cents well spent! It also does a lot better than The Human Fund.

SEINFELD FAN FUN

CHARACTER MOST LIKELY TO BE A BREAD HULK
Kramer

CHARACTER LEAST LIKELY TO BE A BREAD HULK
Jerry

CHARACTER MOST LIKELY TO TAKE UP A CAUSE
RELATED TO BREAD
Elaine

CHARACTER MOST LIKELY TO OWN AN ACTION
FIGURE OF THE INCREDIBLE HULK
Jerry

CHARACTER THAT COULD MANIACALLY SQUEEZE
BREAD
Crazy Joe Davola

REAL WORLD FUN

MORE INFORMATION

- The Incredible Hulk was first published by Marvel Comics in 1962.
- Bread Daily reports that each American consumes, on average, 53 pounds of bread each year.
- Bread Daily says an average slice of packaged bread contains only 1 gram of fat and 75 to 80 calories.
- Assuming one eats a sandwich for breakfast, lunch, and dinner, it would take them 168 days to eat the amount of bread produced from one bushel of wheat, says Bread Daily.
- Bakers Pride says these five countries consume the most bread per person annually:

(1) Turkey: 230 pounds
(2) Bulgaria: 210 pounds
(3) Ukraine: 196 pounds
(4) Greece: 150 pounds
(5) The Netherlands: 137 pounds

15

The Doggie-Style Shoppers

I experimented with a lot of titles for this chapter that included the word "Rover," but in the end, I opened my Seinfeld Eyes and took the low road. Remember when Jerry agreed to babysit a dog for the guy in the hospital? ("The Dog," Season 3, Episode 4). That's what enters my mind when I see dogs in the store.

I love our dog Curly more than 90% of all the humans I've met, but I'm uncomfortable when I see dogs in the grocery store.

In fact, I've been seeing this more and more. What are the rules for bringing a dog to the grocery store? What are the rules for bringing a dog to any type of store? Case in point: My wife recently took Curly to the drugstore. I was a bit surprised, but she said Curly was welcomed with open arms. One of the clerks even said they love it when people bring their dogs to the drugstore. I replied to her using my best TV Show Jerry impersonation of Johnny Carson, "Alright then!"

Back to The Doggie-Style Shoppers, I'm in the store the other day trying to decipher my wife's handwriting, and this woman starts saying, "Sugar Pie, here Sugar Pie." Her dog was huge, probably 150 pounds. Sugar Pie was temporarily off the leash—and lost in the next aisle. I wonder how much damage one of those bigger dogs could do in the dog food aisle. What about the meat section? There's another fun grocery store–related game show just waiting to happen.

Right at the peak of the hellish day-before-Thanksgiving shopping this year, I turned into an aisle to see two ginormous, growling dogs walking down the aisle. They knocked a few cans off the shelf and emitted some deafening barks to confirm their badass status. I'm sure they are good dogs for their owners, but this was a page right out of one of my bad dreams. I flipped around and headed to the next aisle. I had to look behind me the rest of the visit, worried that Thanksgiving was coming early for these dogs, and I was their meal.

How big does a dog have to be before you shouldn't bring it to the grocery store? Our dog is about 22 pounds. Stop laughing, big dog owners. I can hear you. If I brought our dog to the store, she would recognize some of the food in the dog food aisle and start going crazy. This is especially true for the treats. In dog world, there is no such thing as a bad treat. Grocery store managers, want to sell more things to dog lovers? Always put the word "treat" in your ads, and take a clue from the banks and hand out some cheap, generic treats when you see a dog at your place of business.

I read somewhere that these Fido Panderers now rank high on Google searches for dog-friendly restaurants. You don't see cat owners Googling cat-friendly restaurants. I've never seen anybody with their bird at the burger barn.

The parents of a boy in one of my son's former sports teams don't just take their dog to the grocery store, they take their dog everywhere. They even have a special "service dog" vest that the dog wears. I went home and saw that the vest was available on Amazon for $24 and also on three other dog-related websites. I'm guessing that particular dog didn't have any special service dog training, but are you going to be THAT PERSON who publicly challenges someone's service dog status?

As I take you through the "Dog Stuff" section in my diary, I can't close without telling you a pet store / dog wash just moved in next to one of the grocery stores where I shop. They must know more about the correlation between dogs and shopping than the average person. The place looks busy.

SEINFELD FAN FUN

CHARACTER MOST LIKELY TO ENJOY A DOG'S COMPANY
Kramer

CHARACTER MOST LIKELY TO MEET A MAN ON A PLANE AND LATER AGREE TO BABYSIT HIS DOG
Jerry

CHARACTER MOST LIKELY TO GIVE A DOG A CRAZY NAME
Kramer

CHARACTER MOST LIKELY TO BE BITTEN BY A DOG
Newman

CHARACTER MOST LIKELY TO BE AFRAID OF A DOG, EVEN A SMALL DOG
George

CHARACTER MOST LIKELY TO NICKNAME HIMSELF "THE LITTLE BULLDOG"
George

SEINFELD FAN EXTRA CREDIT EXERCISE

Write down the names of at least several *Seinfeld* characters. Next to each one, choose the type of dog that most closely resembles them. It's more fun if you do this with a group of people as you watch "Rochelle, Rochelle."

REAL WORLD FUN

Rover.com listed the Most Popular Puppy Names for 2019:

Top 25 Female Puppy Names
1. Bella
2. Luna
3. Lucy
4. Daisy
5. Lola
6. Sadie
7. Molly
8. Bailey
9. Stella
10. Maggie
11. Sophie
12. Chloe
13. Penny
14. Zoey
15. Lily
16. Coco
17. Roxy
18. Gracie
19. Rosie
20. Nala
21. Ellie
22. Ruby
23. Mia
24. Piper
25. Lilly

. . .

Top 25 Male Puppy Names
1. Max
2. Charlie
3. Cooper
4. Buddy
5. Jack
6. Rocky
7. Duke
8. Bear
9. Oliver
10. Tucker
11. Milo
12. Bentley
13. Toby
14. Leo
15. Teddy
16. Jax
17. Zeus
18. Winston
19. Murphy
20. Louie
21. Jake
22. Ollie
23. Finn
24. Gus
25. Dexter

IT REALLY HAPPENED

One day, after I first moved to Austin in the 90s, and when *Seinfeld* was still airing, I was walking around a track by my apartment. A man walked by with his dog (a black lab). The dog pulled on his leash and tried to run the other way as a car honked in the nearby street.

The man said, "Kramer, settle down! Chill out, Kramer." The

dog settled down in a second. I couldn't resist saying, "Giddy up!" to the man. He smiled and said, "Giddy up!" back to me.

MORE SEINFELD DOG FUN

I feel your vibe. Many of you thought about even more dog-related *Seinfeld* episodes while reading this chapter. You may have thought about "The Andrea Doria," (Season 8, Episode 10) where Kramer takes dog medicine and begins to exhibit the signs of being a dog.

If you're really a hardcore *Seinfeld* fan, you may have thought about *Seinfeld's* pilot episode. In that first episode, Kramer owned a dog named Ralph. It was written into to the episode to correlate with a bit from Jerrry's stand-up. After the dog pounces on George, it is never seen or mentioned in the series again.

16

The Shirt Shockers

*L*ong before I started seeing the grocery store through Seinfeld Eyes, I started understanding that many people wear crazy shirts just to get attention. Based on my diary, this is especially true when it comes to the shirts people choose to wear to the grocery store. As William Shakespeare and Rush say, "All the world's a stage." The Shirt Shockers know they'll have a captive grocery store audience, and they want to bask in all that attention.

Bottom line? Shirts that would get people fired if they wore them to work are freely worn in the grocery store. I feel that I now understand some of the nuances of the grocery store performance world. I frequently wear my Scrantonicity II t-shirt (featuring Kevin Malone on drums) to the grocery store. That's a nod to *The Office*, in case you were confused. I need a new *Seinfeld* t-shirt to add to the mix. The Scrantonicity II shirt not only salutes *The Office*, but also the classic *Synchronicty* album by The Police. It's simultaneously nostalgic and good fun.

Since I started keeping the diary, however, I am amazed (and alarmed) by how many people think it's okay to wear t-shirts with profanity to the grocery store. I know what you're thinking, "Where the hell does Scott shop?" I promise you, the stores I frequent are all in what I consider to be decent neighborhoods where decent people live. Sure, that's a very subjective statement.

In all fairness, most of the craziest t-shirts I am about to mention were seen on my visits to the superstore. There seems to be some unwritten law that the bigger the store, the safer people feel about wearing crazy t-shirts and costumes.

Without further ado, here are some of the shirts that made it into the diary:

Chill the f**k out! (There were no asterisks on the actual shirt)

This person obviously needed everyone to settle down, and they wanted to make sure people knew they really meant it. I especially like the "!" after the verbiage. It would be fun to see Frank Costanza wear one of these shirts. Double *Seinfeld* points if he wears it for Festivus!

Sometimes these shirts are not artful at all, they are just a cry for attention.

F*ck world peace (Notice how there was no exclamation point)

I'm guessing this person is just not a fan of diplomacy. What drives someone to get out of bed and decide that they are going to wear this shirt to the grocery store? I'm guessing that they consider themselves to be, at the very least, a little bit of a gangsta. I could not Google any band names that matched this shirt. As George Costanza would tell you, however, it's all fun and games until a fire breaks out at a party and you have to push your way past kids and a clown to get out of the house ("The Fire," Season 5, Episode 20).

· · ·

Giant Meteor 2020

This was red, white and blue and looked like a shirt for a Presidential candidate. You wear this one when the Republicans, Democrats, Libertarians, Know Nothings, Independents, Socialists, Communists, etc. just don't provide the right platform for your beliefs. I smiled and thought about what that person's face would look like if they suddenly spotted a real meteor about to fall on them. I also wondered how many people it would take to stage a prank where they thought said meteor strike was really happening. Finally, I decided I was too lazy to see the plan through from beginning to end. Besides, the humor that could possibly be squeezed out of such a prank wouldn't be worth all of the work.

OTHER SHIRTS I'VE SEEN AT THE GROCERY STORE:

- **Workin' harder than an ugly stripper** This is also subjective. Besides, why would you willfully choose to pick on ugly strippers? They are people too!
- **Don't be a c**tasaurus** There were no asterisks on the shirt. The lady had a teenager with her. I had to turn away because I was almost positive she was really enjoying the reactions she was getting.
- **Moist** A middle-aged woman was wearing the shirt. There was no indication that she worked for Duncan Hines, or any other baking company.
- **You give my middle finger an erection** This was (surprise surprise!) a college guy getting hot dogs. I'm guessing that if I check the Internet, I will find at least one band named Middle Finger Erection. It's way too many syllables, but on a good day, I can still squeeze the shirt's message into the chorus as I hum Bon Jovi's "You Give Love A Bad Name."

- **You'll all be sorry when I figure out how to breath fire** Teenage girl obviously attending the Khaleesi School of Diplomacy. It's kind of fun—and classier than most of these.
- **What doesn't kill you disappoints me** Older guy with two 12-packs in his cart. I wanted to smile and say, "Underwhelmed much?" but I just walked past and reached for my diary.
- **People... not a big fan.** This could have walked right out of a *Seinfeld* episode.
- **Sorry I'm late, I didn't want to come.** Grandma-looking older lady. If I didn't have the evidence of my own eyes, I would not have placed her in such a shirt. Maybe it was laundry day, and this was her only clean shirt.
- **Harvard Law (back of shirt: Just Kidding)** College-aged guy. I fell for it. I saw the front and thought, "Boy, somebody is pretty proud of their education." I decided there was at least a 50% chance that I would wear a shirt like this if I had also attended Harvard Law. I smiled when I saw the back of the shirt. He got me! Isn't that a lot more fun than "F*ck world peace"?
- **I make beer disappear** He's the Robert "Captain Obvious" Frost of his crew.
- **Bong Hall of Fame** He's Captain Obvious' best friend.
- **If Zombies chase us, I'm totally tripping you** It's pretty funny—and could even be somehow inspired by *Seinfeld* quotes.

FINAL QUESTION:

Besides comfort, why do people love wearing fuzzy slippers and/or pajamas to the store? This question is for another time.

· · ·

SEINFELD FAN FUN

CHARACTER MOST LIKELY TO BE A SHIRT SHOCKER
Morty Seinfeld

CHARACTER LEAST LIKELY TO BE A SHIRT SHOCKER
George

CHARACTER MOST LIKELY TO WEAR A SHIRT
PROMOTING ASTRONAUT PENS
Jack Klompus

CHARACTER MOST LIKELY TO DATE SOMEONE WHO IS
A SHIRT SHOCKER
David Puddy

CHARACTER MOST LIKELY TO BREAK UP WITH
SOMEONE WHO IS A SHIRT SHOCKER
Elaine Marie Benes

REAL WORLD FUN

- I wrote a story, in one of my Fun Stories books, about a lady wearing a Kenny Rogers American Tour 1980 shirt in the grocery store. Was I so profoundly affected by that chance happening, that I have developed this sixth sense related to t-shirts? Probably not. I just need to get a blue #1 Dad t-shirt (like the ones TV Show Jerry bought in Florida) and call the whole t-shirt study a finished project that was hugely enlightening.
- I'm spoiling what was supposed to be a surprise, but I'm going to share that Kenny Rogers grocery store shirt tale

with you as a bonus story at the end of this book. Please act surprised when you see it.

- For whatever reason, when I think about the "F*ck world peace" t-shirt, I sometimes want to listen to the Elvis Costello song "Peace, Love and Understanding." Other times, I need to hear the karaoke version of the song that Bill Murray croons in the movie "Lost In Translation." It's an instant classic and a throwback to his SNL "Nick the Lounge Singer" character.

17

The Fitness Fanatics

Seinfeld's Jimmy is pretty sweet on this one. So is Keith Hernandez. I'm talking about people who turn a grocery store visit into a full-blown workout opportunity.

Your high school coach would tell you there's never a bad time to work out. So, why not do it at the grocery store? I chuckled as I made a diary entry about a guy who was running behind his basket for almost the entirety of his store visit.

"He *really* enjoys running," my TV Show Jerry voice said. I'd love to see George Costanza being told by his boss that he needed to get in a workout while he was at the grocery store.

During the research phase of this book, I observed many types of exercise in the store. I caught a lady doing lunges by the oatmeal section while I was ranting about the fact that they didn't have the larger box of Brown Sugar Cinnamon Pop-Tarts. I imagined that she was punishing herself for eating one of those sugary cereals in the nearby shelves.

Once upon a time, my grandma's doctor advised her that she could use canned goods as hand weights. I was fairly young then and thought that was very funny. Now, it seems like the hipster thing to do when people buy canned goods. I have seen several people give these canned babies a cursory curl (or three) before putting them into the basket.

Headbands and wristbands seem to pop up more at the grocery store than any other place, except gyms. Have you ever worn a headband to the grocery store like The Inspiration? I have not done so, but I have worn wristbands to the store because I had been coaching a Little League Baseball practice at the time. Of course, you coach better—and probably shop better—wearing wristbands.

Either I'm slowing down, or there are now speed walkers at the store on many of my visits. I don't see them buy things. But I do see them looking at their watches and checking their pulse a lot. One guy even brought a clipboard to record his heart rate. But he looked very healthy, not like he had health issues that needed charting. Bottom line? If you chart your health stats on a clipboard while shopping at the store, you are pretty serious about working out.

One day, I created a log in my diary because I saw a store employee stocking the shelf while sitting on one of those big exercise balls. It was about 8 pm. I'm guessing the night supervisor at the store was not as strict as the daytime supervisor. I've not seen it again. Perhaps it was a triple dog dare? Imagine getting in trouble for a rogue exercise ball!

Years ago, I used to think it was cute when my grandma and some ladies from her church started a club that exercised by walking at the mall. They even had red shirts that said, in white letters, "Mall Walking Team."

True confession time. While I stop short of wearing headphones or an exercise suit—or one of those crazy miner-inspired headband lights that early-morning joggers wear—I think I may be counted in the group of people who lists the grocery store as a place to exercise.

It's part of my new workout routine. Recently, I cancelled our family's gym membership. It's because the "free month" and "great yearly discount" offers that I had once skillfully combined had now morphed into a growing bill that totaled nearly $90 per month. On top of that, we're also paying more for bread now. Walking is mostly free (unless you buy one of those smart treadmills that communicate with online fitness instructors in 37 languages), and our trusty dog

Curly is now my fitness instructor. She can successfully get me to walk far more often than any high-dollar gym tyrant.

I'm okay with being called a card-carrying member of The Fitness Fanatics. I use an app on my phone that keeps track of the miles I walk. I set yearly goals. When grocery store shopping, I will now often choose the largest store in my vicinity because that means I will get more walking done around the store. In fact, I will sometimes skip an item on my list just to be able to circle back later and complete another fraction of a mile on the app.

The Fitness Fanatic workout starts in the grocery store parking lot. I carefully park an entire zip code away from the store and then locate a basket as far away from the store as possible. Why don't 5k competitions partner with these big stores?

Because I Google so many things that one of my nicknames is "The Freakin' Michael Phelps of Googling," I had to see what Google had to say about grocery stores and fitness. As it was, Google said a lot. Fitness Magazine had extensive details on the ShopRite of Greater Morristown in New Jersey that has its own Health and Wellness Clubs, complete with a resident registered dietician, a cosmetologist, and classes in Zumba, barre and yoga.

As far back as 2011, Whole Foods launched Wellness Centers in five of its locations. Other locations offer fitness classes through partnerships with local gyms.

Solo offered a grocery store workout routine to use in its stores. The routine starts with a lap around the store for warm up and then goes on to detail Good Cart Posture, Top Shelf Stretches, Lower Shelf Squats, Produce Calf Raises, Waiting-In-Line Leg Lifts, and Grocery Bag Arm Lifts. Solo invites you to "think outside the gym" and make the world your exercise studio. My Seinfeld Mind heard "think outside the gym" in a very enthusiastic Kramer voice.

SEINFELD FAN FUN

CHARACTER MOST LIKELY TO EXERCISE IN THE GROCERY STORE

Kramer

CHARACTER LEAST LIKELY TO EXERCISE IN THE
GROCERY STORE
Jerry

CHARACTER MOST LIKELY TO TRY AND INVENT A
NEW SHOE THAT IS SPECIFICALLY DESIGNED FOR
EXCERICSING IN THE GROCERY STORE
Kramer

CHARACTER MOST LIKELY TO GO ON AN EXERCISING
DATE IN THE GROCERY STORE
Elaine

CHARACTER YOU DO NOT WANT TO SEE PARTICI-
PATING IN A GROCERY STORE EXERCISE DANCE CLASS
Elaine

CHARACTER MOST LIKELY TO GET HURT EXERCISING
IN THE GROCERY STORE
Jimmy

REAL WORLD FUN

MORE INFORMATION

- Statista says that in 2017, U.S. fitness centers had a total membership of 60.87 million people.
- The percentage of people in the U.S. who belong to a health club has increased 10% over the last three years.
- Statista says there are about 36,000 membership-based exercise facilities in the United States.
- The CDC says only 20.6% of people—including 23% of all men surveyed and 18% of all women surveyed—meet the recommended requirement for exercise.

- The CDC says the people most likely to exercise are between the ages of 18 and 24; those people make up almost 31% of all exercisers.
- Statista says that globally, more than 170 million people are members of a health/fitness club.

18

The Hillbilly Shoppers

*B*esides The Hillbilly Shoppers, I also like to call this next group of people The Hippies. No matter what you call them, they like to traipse around the store without their shoes. Is this even legal?

Right off the bat, I must confess that I do not enjoy being without shoes—not even in my own house. My wife laughs because I like to put on topsiders just to sit on the couch and watch *Seinfeld* re-runs.

It's okay if you love to spend half your life not wearing shoes. There's nothing wrong with that. What I don't like, however, is seeing people in the grocery store without shoes.

The grocery store is the place where we buy our fruits and vegetables. People have worked long hot days in fields in the Midwest and on dairy farms as far as Wisconsin to make sure we have lots of different food choices. The end game is basically all about getting a lot of nutritional items. What does any of that have to do with bare feet?

No comments please, foot fetishizers.

NOTE: I stopped noting this hillbilly activity after I had recorded it five times in my grocery diary. Yuck!

I'm guessing that people who don't wear shoes at the grocery store do it to show how carefree they are, but then my Seinfeld Eyes have to fixate on the fact that they are barefooted. I worry if I see sharp corners on aisle displays. I worry they'll get a foot injury if a cart gets too close to them. They're wallowing in grocery store freedom, and I'm a wreck worrying about their safety.

The minute I spot people not wearing shoes, I have to stare at their feet to try and determine how dirty they are from walking around sans shoes. If I see really dirty feet, I have to back off about 15–20 feet and observe the things they are touching. I don't want to touch the same things. Their hands might be cleaner than mine, but the dirty feet make me leery of everything they are doing. I can't explain that logic.

I once saw one of the dads from my Little League Baseball team in the store. We shook hands, had a quick conversation and then he walked away. I suddenly noticed he wasn't wearing shoes. Why? I had to stash my cart, go to the restroom and wash my hands. I'm hoping he knows several other dads who shop without shoes, so he doesn't realize I am talking about him.

In a related story, these Hillbilly Shoppers usually have the carry-along basket. It's rare to see someone with a full-on cart and bare feet. Just as they can't be bothered by the burden of wearing shoes, they also need a lighter cart so they can fully enjoy their Hill-billy ways.

Male or female—and it is usually females when I spot Hillbilly shoppers—the song "Thank God I'm A Country Boy" by John Denver enters my head. Like the song says, "Life ain't nothing but a funny, funny riddle!"

SEINFELD FAN FUN

CHARACTER MOST LIKELY TO BE A HILLBILLY
SHOPPER
Elaine

CHARACTER LEAST LIKELY TO BE A HILLBILLY
SHOPPER
George

CHARACTER MOST LIKELY TO ASSOCIATE WITH A
PACK OF HILBILLY SHOPPERS
Kramer

CHARACTER MOST LIKELY TO WALK BAREFOOT AS
THEY FOLLOW THE GRATEFUL DEAD AROUND THE
COUNTRY
Dr. Tim Whatley

CHARACTER MOST LIKELY TO STEAL SOMETHING AS
THEY ARE BEING A HILLBILLY SHOPPER
Uncle Leo

REAL WORLD FUN

First Hand Account

The Hillbilly Shopping Universe spoke to me the other day. I had recently seen comedian Sebastian Maniscalco do a show here in Austin. He has this great routine about going to other people's houses where they have a rule that you must take off your shoes. There you are, meeting people in your sock feet and trying to make small talk. Check out Sebastian's routine when you get a chance.

Anyway, I'm smiling about Sebastian's show and I see a guy walk up right to the grocery store entrance, kick off his shoes, place them neatly against the wall, and enter the store in his sock feet. I made a funny face and did a triple-take. It was like the old days in gym class when we had to put our shoes against the wall before playing on the mat in our sock feet.

My mind went Kramer. "He's going in, Jerry! (WAVERING VOICE) In his sock feet. Poor little pinkie toe!"

I wanted to follow Mr. Sock Feet around and ask a few questions for my diary, but I refrained from doing so. I decided nothing he said would be better than my initial experience of seeing him leave his shoes outside the store and then saunter through the front door in his sock feet.

Full confession: I also wanted to hide his shoes and shoot a funny video, but I did not do that. For once, I realized that was the ghost of College Scott speaking to me in a prank-laden language that I no longer recognize (most days).

EXTRA CREDIT:

Come up with your own reasons as to why Mr. Sock Feet left his shoes neatly against the wall before he entered the store. Please send them to the Fun Stories Series Facebook page or e-mail them to me at randymidnite512@yahoo.com.

19

The Headphone Jones

I learn the most amazing things when I write books. I love popular music and you already know that I grew up listening to Casey Kasem's *American Top 40* countdowns each week. FYI, Casey is my all-time favorite storyteller. This next item reads like something he would share on one of his weekly countdowns.

I also like Cheech & Chong. Their humor is fun and unique. I have listened to many of their albums and laughed at many of their movies. Did you know that Cheech & Chong once had a song called "Basketball Jones?" It's a parody of "Love Jones" by The Brighter Side of Darkness.

Because of my crazy pop culture associations, this song enters my mind anytime I see people shopping in the grocery store wearing headphones and earbuds. My Seinfeld Eyes first zeroed in on head-phones when I saw The Inspiration, but now earbuds (wireless and wired) and over-the-ear headphones pop up during nearly all of my grocery store trips.

I collectively call all of these ear-plugged folks "Headphone Jones" or just "Jonesey."

I recently told my son, "Jonesey over there is really cranking out the jams and dancing with that cart." My son thought I might have finally hit the point where my elevator does not ever make it to the top floor.

Many of these Headphones Jones types also sing loudly as they shop. Have they discovered the secret of life? Are they anti-social? Are they just so involved in their music that they can't break away from their tunes, not even during their supermarket trip? Is there a chance that any of them are listening to Matt and Vinnie on the *Seincast* podcast? If you love going over every little detail of *Seinfeld*, please check out that podcast.

I recently got some name brand headphones I'll call "Eats"— the big, over-the-ear kind. I sometimes wear my Eats as I walk around our block. Make no mistake, I'm the Headphone Jones of my block. For whatever reason, I can't bring myself to wear my Eats in the grocery store. I wasn't raised that way.

Please post pictures to any of my social media sites if you are the Headphone Jones of your crew. My ultimate goal might be to wear my Eats in the grocery store on Sunday night as I switch out smashed pieces of bread to build one really good loaf.

SEINFELD FAN FUN

CHARACTER MOST LIKELY TO BE HEADPHONE JONES
Kramer

CHARACTER LEAST LIKELY TO BE HEADPHONE JONES
Elaine

CHARACTER MOST LIKELY TO BE ANNOYED BY HEAD-PHONE JONES
George

CHARACTER THAT WILL TRY THE HEADPHONE JONES METHOD OF SHOPPING IF IT MIGHT ATTRACT A DATE
Jerry

CHARACTER MOST LIKELY TO PUT A HEADPHONE
JONES PRODUCT IN A CATALOG
J Peterman

CHARACTER THAT CAN BEST HELP YOU IF YOUR EARS
ARE DAMAGED BY YOUR HEADPHONE JONES ACTIVITY
Jackie Chiles

REAL WORLD FUN

MORE INFORMATION

- The song "Basketball Jones" by Cheech and Chong reached #15 on the Billboard Hot 100.
- It's the only spoof song to peak higher than the original.
- Speaking of Casey Kasem, I learned some extra trivia about "Basketball Jones." Did you know that one of the Beatles is on the recording? Yep, George Harrison played guitar on the track.
- What's more, there are several other legendary music industry folks on the record.
- That's Carole King on background vocals.
- Tom Scott plays the saxophone on the song.
- Billy Preston played the organ on the record.
- The "cheerleaders" on the record are Michelle Phillips, Ronnie Spector, Fanita James and Darlene Love.

20

The Scooby Doo Shoppers

*J*erry has this running gag on the show where he answers the phone and hears a distressed / upset / frazzled / needy / all-of-the-above George on the other end of the line. Jerry gets a wicked smile and says smugly, "Who is this?"

That's part of the inspiration for something I say when I see oddly dressed people at the grocery store. I like to say, "Where are you?" in a TV Show Jerry voice and call these people "Scooby Doo Shoppers."

If you don't immediately recognize the reference, the other characters in the *Scooby Doo* cartoons, especially Shaggy, would often say, "Scooby Doo, where are you?" Also, the villains in *Scooby Doo* would often wear outlandish costumes and masks. At the end of the show, the culprits would often be unmasked.

As you know, I embrace the weird, the wild, the wonderful, and the wacky. I'm amused by fuzzy slippers and weird hats—especially those Dr. Seuss-style hats—when I see them in the grocery store. I enjoy seeing people in full baseball uniforms in the store—just kids. I don't mind bowling shoes—if they have the actual size of the shoe on the back of them. If you wear no shoes, then of course, you are a Hillbilly Shopper. We've also talked about The Shirt Shockers.

The Scooby Doo Shoppers are a different breed. They throw caution to the wind and don't worry about embarrassing themselves or their family. My diary entries included backwards shirts, two different shoes, and shorts with holes in unfortunate places that you know should not be seen in public. I called one entry "Madonna" because this middle-aged woman wore just her bra as the top accompanying her jeans. I saw that one, shook my head, and wished I hadn't.

Where are you? The grocery store is not Summer Theater Camp.

Even if you own a big SpongeBob head, you don't have to wear it to the store. Now, if the store is selling said SpongeBob head, have at it. That's funny. Just don't bring your own big head to the grocery store. That seems like part of the plot of a low-budget horror movie.

I've flip-flopped on a football siting from earlier in the year. At first I didn't think it was funny that a middle-aged guy was wearing full-length pads and an old helmet, and was carrying a football like a running back. I labeled it a cry for attention. Your interpretations may vary. I'm thinking he lost at poker, or was involved in a Truth Or Dare game as part of his class reunion weekend.

Where are you?

I'm now convinced, however, that there's some kind of subculture out there that gets game points for shopping in ridiculous attire. My diary entries have included numerous people wearing robes and pajamas to the store. It included several shirtless men. I expected these entries to include softball uniforms on middle-aged men. What I underlined in the entry was the fact that they were wearing metal cleats. The store must love that. Next to the entry, I drew a smiley face and noted that they were buying a lot of beer.

One day, I saw Spider-Man in full costume in the frozen foods section. He was not the Spider-McFly whom I had mentioned earlier in the book. We were several months away from Halloween. His mask was too small. He had no kids with him. He was 40 years old if he was a day. My Seinfeld Eyes could not look away.

Where are you, Scooby Doo?

Some people can get labeled a Scooby Doo Shopper, just

because of their "normal" weirdness. Other than Eddie Van Halen, who carries their guitar around the store? I'm not too familiar with the dance world, but was it okay that I saw tap shoes—on an older woman with gray hair?

Where are you?

"Where are you" took on a new meaning a couple of weeks ago. At the big superstore, Griff and I were sneaking 17 items into the self-checkout area that is set aside for shoppers with 15 items or less. I once wrote a whole story about Grocery Store Math as part of the *Fun Stories* book series. I used to be pretty uptight about people who go over the 15-item limit, but I'm a little more relaxed about it now. This is especially true at the superstore because they have a large area with about a dozen or so of these checkout stations. Don't worry, I'm still uptight about breaking the limit at the regular grocery store.

While we were ringing up the items, and I was swinging the pricing gun like Pete Townshend playing his signature, windmill-style guitar, Griff spotted something and whispered to me. When I looked, there was a group of 4-5 folks that I eventually called "The Bizarro Bunnies" standing at the checkout area two stations behind us.

This was not a Schmoopie-related thing—at least I don't think so. They had purple paint on their faces, fur glued onto sweatshirts, cotton balls on their noses, and they made weird intermittent noises rather than talking. The noises resembled the snorting sound of a pig mixed with goat sounds and a sheep baa.

Where are you?

My first five thoughts were:

1. This is some kind of prelude to a robbery, and these purple bunnies are about to stage a well-planned diversion to distract people from their counterparts who'd make a run for it with stolen items. There is definitely a van outside with fake license plates, waiting to whisk them all away.

. . .

2. This group is attending some type of animal costume fetish sex convention. They've come here from all over the world to reinforce Austin's unofficial motto of "Keep Austin Weird." These noises are foreplay. They barely know each other. They need some snacks and "other items" to break the ice and make the weekend convention run more smoothly.

3. The aliens among us are finally showing themselves—and it's far scarier than we all imagined.

4. I've somehow forgotten that it is Halloween week, and the parties have started without me. I'm going to need numerous bags of candy for trick-or-treaters, plus a few that are just for me.

5. With all of the purple paint, this may be some type of tribute to Prince. Upon further review, this might be the worst face-and-body paint job that I have ever seen. I'm not a big fan of the color purple, but I think Minnesota Vikings fans everywhere would be shocked to see this subpar display.

For fun, you might consider ranking the likelihood of my five theories above. At the time, I would have ranked them in the sequence in which I thought them up, but now I might rank the first two about even. I'm still unclear as to whether I was observing males, females, or a mix of the two when we saw The Bizarro Bunnies.

Their example was just what I needed to tie up this story . Griff and I left while the Bizarros were still making their noises and taking a lot of time to ring up their items. If I had to do it all over again, I would have paid closer attention to what they were buying.

The whole incident made me think again, in the TV Show Jerry voice, "Where are you?"

· · ·

SEINFELD FAN FUN

MOST LIKELY TO BE A SCOOBY DOO SHOPPER
David Puddy

LEAST LIKELY TO BE A SCOOBY DOO SHOPPER
Elaine

MOST LIKELY TO GET FREAKED OUT WHEN THEY SEE
A SCOOBY DOO SHOPPER
George

MOST LIKELY TO COMMENT ABOUT A SCOOBY DOO
SHOPPER
Jerry

MOST LIKELY TO THINK A SCOOBY DOO SHOPPER
NEEDS TREATMENT
Estelle Costanza

MOST LIKELY TO HAVE A CRAZIER LICENSE PLATE
THAN A SCOOBY DOO SHOPPER
Dr. Howard Cooperman (The Ass Man)

REAL WORLD FUN

- As many of you may know—either you knew it already, or you learned it in one of my *Fun Stories* books—Casey Kasem played the role of Shaggy in the *Scooby Doo* cartoons. It's so cool that he was the one who often got to say, "Scooby Doo, where are you?"
- The first *Scooby Doo* cartoon was produced in 1969. I'm thinking we missed a big opportunity for a national

holiday complete with a parade by not declaring the 50th anniversary of *Scooby Doo* a national holiday.

- Scooby is a Great Dane.
- Do you know the full names of the characters on *Scooby Doo*? They are Fred Jones, Velma Dinkley, Daphne Blake, and Norville "Shaggy" Rogers.
- According to Google, the most popular Halloween costumes for 2019 were:

- It
- Witch
- Spider-Man
- Dinosaur
- Descendants
- Clown
- Fortnite
- Chucky
- 1980s
- Unicorn

21

The Soul Crushers

*Y*ou're having a perfectly good day. You wander into the store and extend a "Hello, how are you?" to another human being in an attempt to add a little sunshine to their day. Then, that other human being unloads all of their troubles on you. It can be soul crushing. You go from sunshine, unicorns, and rainbows to dodging life's lightning bolts and hailstorms. You start wondering whether that person's negativity could soon engulf your own life.

Has this happened to you? I call these people The Soul Crushers. There are Intentional Soul Crushers and Unintentional Soul Crushers. The Intentional Soul Crushers are the worst. The following is an account from when I met an Intentional Soul Crusher a couple of years ago before I even started keeping my *Seinfeld Eyes* grocery journal.

PLEASE WIGGLE YOUR HEAD OR WIGGLE YOUR FINGERS TO MAKE SURE YOU UNDERSTAND WE ARE FLASHING BACK TO A COUPLE OF YEARS. MY MIND IMMEDIATELY GOES TO WAYNE AND GARTH FROM

WAYNE'S WORLD. I WIGGLE MY HANDS UP AND DOWN AND SAY "DOOTLE-E-DO, DOOTLE-E-DO" IN A HIGH-PITCHED VOICE TO MIMIC THEIR DISSOLVE FLASH-BACK TECHNIQUE.

Helloooooo. ("The Voice," Season 9, Episode 2) I'm in the store trudging down one of my favorite aisles—the one with the potato chips, tortilla chips, corn chips, and Triscuits. I have just figured out that there are like 10 different types of Triscuits now.

Little do I know that it is about to get even weirder in Triscuit World.

I see a seemingly pleasant older man who is smartly dressed in a black sweater and black beret. I squint a bit and imagine this is what Robin Williams might look like if he were still alive today. It's such a pleasant little vision full of "Nanoo, nanoo," and "Good morning, Viet Naaaaaaam" sounds in my mind. All of this makes me warm and happy inside, but it also makes me far more susceptible to soul crushing.

Here's how it plays out...

ME: Hello. Good to see you. How are you today, sir?

SOUL CRUSHER: Well, I'm not a bit good. The hip replacement didn't take. I can barely walk.

ME: I'm really sorry to hear that. My dad had a hip replacement, and he said it can be tough.

SOUL CRUSHER: My dog got hit by a car last week.

· · ·

ME: That is so tough. I know you probably loved your dog as much as our family loves our dog. You have my condolences.

SOUL CRUSHER: I'm peeing a lot of blood.

ME: Ouch. This is just not your day. Do you need to see a doctor? Do I need to call somebody to help you? What can we do to help you?

SOUL CRUSHER: No doctors. They try to take all of my money. I got laid off at work, and had to retire. They want to put me in a home.

ME: All of this is so unfortunate. Are you shopping with somebody?

SOUL CRUSHER: My son didn't call me on Father's Day.

ME (PANICKING): What can we do to make your day a little brighter?

SOUL CRUSHER: Maybe a hooker? I really like Asian women.

ME: What?

SOUL CRUSHER'S WIFE COMES WALKING UP

. . .

SOUL CRUSHER (WHISPERS): Never mind.

WIFE: You're not bothering this man, are you, Eugene?

SOUL CRUSHER: I'm just trying to get my cracked pepper Triscuits, and this man's asking me all sorts of questions.

WIFE: Oh no!

ME: It seems like he's having a tough day. I'm just trying to help.

WIFE: Did he talk about peeing blood?

ME (AWKWARD): Yes

WIFE: Shame on you, Eugene! (HITS HIM SOFTLY)

WIFE (TO ME): He hates talking to strangers. It brings out his twisted sense of humor.

ME: Good one, Eugene. That was soul crushing. You have a gift.

SOUL CRUSHER: Yeah, yeah. Mind your own business next time. Can I get my Triscuits now?

. . .

This incident really felt like it was straight out of a *Seinfeld* episode. It brought to mind the episode where Elaine gets the gang to volunteer by visiting the elderly, each "adopting" an old person (Season 4, Episode 18, "The Old Man"). Elaine gets freaked out by hers, George gets fired by his guy, and Jerry loses his guy. Kramer and Newman scheme to steal records from Jerry's guy and sell them to a vintage music store.

The Soul Crusher really drew me in with his particular style of comedy. He kept dumping more of his problems on me and making me feel escalating levels of sorry for him.

The whole incident was soul crushing for me—then, when I found out he was lying and playing me for a fool, it was soul crushing in a completely different way. Sometimes a random person can smile at you and brighten your day. Other times, The Soul Crusher steps in and spreads cumulonimbus clouds all over your world. Thank you, Hurricane Eugene.

Final note, I always wanted to meet Robin Williams. His comedy could be so wonderfully wild, wacky and weird. After this experience, I feel like I at least got the chance to see a fairly decent Robin Williams cover act.

SEINFELD FAN FUN

CHARACTER MOST LIKELY TO BE A SOUL CRUSHER
Kramer

CHARACTER MOST LIKELY TO EAT PEZ WHILE
TALKING TO A SOUL CRUSHER
Jerry

VEHICLE MOST LIKELY TO BE DRIVEN BY A SOUL
CRUSHER
The Cougar 9000

CHARACTER MOST LIKELY TO FIGHT CHILDREN IN THE STORE IF THEY ARE SOUL CRUSHERS
Kramer

REAL WORLD FUN

MORE INFORMATION

- I sometimes listen to topic-appropriate music as I write these stories. It fuels the creative process.
- In some instances, I make a playlist of topic-appropriate songs that also includes a song that is the exact opposite of the sentiment being expressed in the other songs.
- I call that song the "Flip the Script" song.
- That's what happened here.
- I made a playlist of five songs that played over and over as I wrote this story:

"Bonecrusher" by Soulhat
"Maxwell's Silver Hammer" by The Beatles
"Mean Mr. Mustard" by The Beatles
"Dirty Deeds Done Dirt Cheap" by AC/DC
"We Are The World" by USA For Africa
(*This one is obviously the Flip the Script song*)

22

The Make-Believe Marys

*Y*ou trust your GPS to give you great directions and get you where you need to go for business meetings, family trips, snack runs, etc. What if your GPS went haywire and/or turned on you? That's sort of what happened in the incident recorded in this next diary entry.

I'd like to tell you about Make-Believe Mary, or some might call her Fake Direction Fannie. Or The Fake GPS. Or The Bogus Direction-Giver. Can you tell she is still weighing on my mind? Any way you look at it, she lives in the neighborhood of make-believe, but she is not a friend of Fred Rogers.

Even though I love all of the items the super-size grocery stores can sell, it is sometimes difficult to find an exact item on my grocery list. On particularly bad days, I've unsuccessfully circled the store several times trying to find the last item left on my list. It's even made me do something I hadn't considered before. I've put aside male pride and asked a store clerk for directions. On this particular day, it didn't work out how I had expected.

The store had undergone a makeover. The store app said my favorite brand of taco seasoning was on aisle 8. It was not there. I spotted a teenage store employee in a red smock. I smiled and asked her where I could find the taco seasoning. Without hesitation, she told me to head to aisle 10. I was quite impressed that out of all of the thousands of items in the store, she instantly knew that taco seasoning lived on aisle 10. When I arrived at aisle 10, however, there were potholders and bowls and spoons and such, but there was no taco seasoning. It turns out that Make-Believe Mary had just randomly given me a fake aisle number for taco seasoning to get me to move along and quit bothering her.

It's all part of a bigger plot. I lightly thumped my noggin to take back all of the praise I had given her in my mind. Frank Costanza has his move. Make-Believe Mary used her FAKE GPS MOVE on me.

Later in the trip, I saw her again. Make-Believe Mary kind of smirked when she saw me. I was ready for her. I had looked up on the store's mobile app that charcoal lives on aisle 9. I asked her, "Excuse me, I wonder if I could bother you again for the location of the charcoal?"

Make-Believe Mary pleasantly (and quickly) replied that it was on aisle 11. I was on to her system. Aisle 11 was one more than the aisle 10 answer she had given me for the taco seasoning. As she started to smirk again and walk away, I said, "Excuse me, but your mobile app says that charcoal is on aisle 9?"

But Make-Believe Mary had played this bogus direction game so long that she didn't even get flustered. She said, "That's right. We moved it last week when we did that store evaluation with the consultants."

I looked at her and said, in my best TV Show Jerry voice, "Oh, you're good. But you should use that brain to help change the world, not the location of the charcoal and the taco seasoning. Wouldn't you feel better if you really helped people?"

Not the least bit phased, she just laughed and walked away. I'm almost positive she said "Old people" in a half-cough under her breath. Half-cough talking is a subject for another day, but make no mistake—I am not a fan of it.

.   .   .

SEINFELD FAN FUN

CHARACTER MOST LIKELY TO BE A FAKE GPS
Elaine

CHARACTER MOST LIKELY TO FALL VICTIM TO A
FAKE GPS
Jerry

CHARACTER MOST LIKELY TO PUT THEIR OWN VOICE
ON THE GPS (OR ON MOVIEFONE)
Kramer

CHARACTER THAT COULD RECORD THE MEANEST
GPS MESSAGES
The Soup Nazi

CHARACTER MOST LIKELY TO ASK MAKE-BELIEVE
MARY ABOUT ENVELOPES
Susan Ross

REAL WORLD FUN

MORE INFORMATION

- My sons and niece once mischievously changed my mom's car GPS system to Japanese. It was a pretty good prank, but then they forgot to change it back before both of our families went home after the holidays. It was not my mom's favorite grandchild moment.
- As I write this, Waze recently began offering a Cookie Monster voice choice. First, it was fun to hear Cookie Monster say silly things and even ask if we should offer cookies to the police. Then, it became clear that the Cookie Monster voice was still being developed. It didn't

have some of the features many folks like me treasure—
such as street names. Lately, however, I must say it is
getting better. If you're in a bad mood, get the Cookie
Monster voice for Waze.

- According to Wikipedia, the Global Positioning System
  (GPS)—originally NAVSTAR GPS—is a satellite-based
  radio navigation system owned by the United States
  government and operated by the United States Air
  Force.
- It is a global navigation satellite system that provides
  geolocation and time information to a GPS receiver
  anywhere on or near the Earth where there is an
  unobstructed line of sight to four or more GPS satellites.
- The GPS project was launched by the U.S. Department
  of Defense in 1973 for the United States military and
  became fully operational in 1995.
- It was made available for civilian use in the 1980s.
- According to Statista, 54% of people aged 18–64 used
  their cell phones for maps/GPS navigation during the
  four-week period prior to a 2018 study.
- Statista says that there were 1,886 active artificial
  satellites orbiting the earth as of April 30, 2018, with 859
  of them belonging to the United States. The nearest
  competitor, China, had just 250 of them.
- I'm seriously thinking someone was goofing on me, but
  the taco seasoning changed locations three different
  times at this particular store during my diary entry
  period.

23

The Talk Show Hosts

*O*ne of my all-time favorite episodes of *Seinfeld* is "The Merv Griffin Show" (Season 9, Episode 6). In the episode, Kramer finds the old set pieces from the Merv Griffin Show in a dumpster, drags them into his apartment, and starts acting out an imaginary program where he is the talk show host. It's pretty far-fetched, but sign me up for this wild ride!

On the other side of the coin, one of my least favorite things to experience in the grocery store is The Talk Show Host. The Talk Show Host is someone who talks to you the whole time you are in line and just does not stop talking. You usually encounter a Talk Show Host when you are at least six-deep in line behind the checkout stand. This allows for 10–15 minutes of Talk Show Host stories.

There you are, trying to play a game on your phone or text with your wife or write crazy things in your Grocery Store Diary, and they won't stop talking. Smiles and carefully inserted phrases like "uh huh," "yes," "that's right," and "that's cool" don't hold up against this tyrant talker. Sure, you feel a little bad about being annoyed because they're usually a really nice person, but The Talk Show Host just keeps yammering.

Soon, they're several levels deep into their story, and you are completely lost. At first, they were talking about their son. Now, they're talking about their son's wife's boss's daughter—and they want your opinion on something you haven't fully heard or understood.

What do you do?

Start by shaking your head and making eye contact. Do not get pinned down on a "yes" or "no" answer. You don't want to be responsible for some kid you don't know not getting asked to prom because a random person (you) in the grocery store said she really didn't even need braces.

Simply reply, "I'm probably not the best person to respond to that question. That's more of a family thing." If that doesn't work, ask them what they think is the right thing to do, and be better prepared to pay more attention next time.

To be better prepared, keep a "Get Out of Talk Show Host Free Card" in your wallet. If you have the card, simply hand it to The Talk Show Host.

Of course, I'm not literally asking you to print out a card that says "Get Out of Talk Show Host Free." The card might be a store coupon that you hand them as a distraction. Coupons expire. For better results, keep one of those customer satisfaction survey cards in your wallet that grocery stores stock at the customer service counter.

If you have a better idea, please share it on one of the Fun Stories social media sites, or e-mail it to me so that I can share it with our group.

I once had to spend a full 10 minutes with a Talk Show Host on a Saturday morning, and then I saw her again just ahead of me as I was entering the store for a quick trip on Monday night. I tiptoed like Austin Powers around the store to avoid another conversation. Then I followed her at a safe distance and waited for her to enter a checkout line. I chose a checkout line about four rows over and then waved when we made eye contact—as she was in full Talk Show Host mode with the lady behind her. I then safely spent the next several minutes writing about the experience in my dairy.

. . .

SEINFELD FAN FUN

CHARACTER MOST LIKELY TO BE A TALK SHOW HOST
Kramer (Merv Griffin)

CHARACTER LEAST PATIENT WITH A TALK
SHOW HOST
Jerry

CHARACTER THAT WOULD BE MOST FLATTERED TO
BE ASKED TO BE ON A TALK SHOW
Elaine

GUESTS I'D MOST LIKE TO SEE ON KRAMER'S
VERSION OF THE MERV GRIFFIN SHOW
• Bob Sacamano
• Cousin Jeffrey
• Jerry's Sister
• Bobby "Poor Little" Pinkus
• Corky Ramirez
• Dr. Bison
• Lomez
• Arthur Pensky
• Jay Riemenschneider
• The Lopper (Son of Dad)
• Hand Model Ray McKigney

CHARACTER MOST LIKELY TO GET ON A TALK SHOW
BY CREATING A COFFEE TABLE BOOK OF COFFEE
TABLES
Kramer

REAL WORLD FUN

MORE INFORMATION

- The Merv Griffin Show began in 1962 on NBC. It later ran on CBS. Its syndicated version lasted until September 1986.
- Rick Moranis (Bob McKenzie) played Merv Griffin on the SCTV parody of the show.
- The Seinfeld episode "The Merv Griffin Show" first aired on November 6, 1997.
- Merv Griffin created *Wheel of Fortune*. It first aired on January 6, 1975. Chuck Woolery was the first host of the show. Pat Sajak began hosting in 1981. Vanna White joined the show in 1982.
- *The Tonight Show Starring Johnny Carson* had frequent guest hosts, sometimes for entire weeks during Johnny's vacations.
- Eight people guest-hosted more than 50 times during the first 21 years of the show's run:

Joey Bishop: 177 times
Joan Rivers: 93 times
John Davidson: 87 times
Bob Newhart: 87 times
David Brenner: 70 times
McLean Stevenson: 58 times
Jerry Lewis: 52 times
David Letterman: 51 times

24

The Amphibians

*T*his next diary entry requires a leap of faith from you. Trust me, it's pretty amusing once you give it a chance. The Amphibians are people who push two carts at once in the grocery store.

What?

Okay, here's how we get here. A person who can do things equally well with both their hands is ambidextrous. Over the years, however, at least several athletes, including college basketball player Charles Shackleford, have confused this term and incorrectly stated in media interviews that they are "amphibious." That's good fun. It's a magnificent example of malapropism. That's where you misuse a word that sounds similar to another word. It's especially funny when these interviewees hold up both hands as they say "amphibious."

Now focus your Seinfeld Eyes, and take the leap with me.

That's why I call people with two carts "The Amphibians." Like this term or hate it, it is always interesting to see a person trying to push two grocery baskets at the same time. It's right out of the Frank Costanza Feats of Strength items in the Festivus Episode of *Seinfeld* ("The Strike," Season 9, Episode 10). I only observed

Amphibians twice during the diary research period, but they were glorious both times!

With a tip of the cap to all of Jerry's great appearances on *The Late Show With David Letterman*, here are the Top 10 Reasons The Amphibians Need Two Baskets:

NUMBER TEN

They have 15 kids and are frantically working to catch up to the Duggars. This requires at least 25 gallons of milk a week.

NUMBER NINE

They own an identical grocery store as this one. They come to this grocery store to buy one of everything, then mark up the price by 15%, and sell all of the items in their own store.

NUMBER EIGHT

Two words: booster club. They missed the last meeting at their high school and now they've been tasked with buying 300 hamburger patties, 400 bottles of water, and 500 packages of Skittles.

NUMBER SEVEN

They're on the Michael Phelps Training Program.

NUMBER SIX

The second basket is there for spare parts in case the first basket blows a handle or loses a wheel.

NUMBER FIVE

They are following the Miss America Pageant Rules while shopping. The second basket will assume the title of the first basket if the first basket is unable to carry out its duties—or in case it's found that the first basket once posed nude in an inappropriate basket magazine.

NUBER FOUR

They live 150 miles from the store and only shop once a month. They have sworn loyalty to the store's owners and never shop anywhere else.

NUMBER THREE

They own a freezer business that lets them stock up on sale items, save lots of money, and then use that extra money to feed their bingo addiction.

NUMBER TWO

They are secret shopper spies for another store. The last thing this store would expect a shopping spy to do would be to shop with two baskets.

NUMBER ONE

They've been in a coma for a year, and now they are very hungry.

No matter what you think about The Amphibians, the first thing somebody says to a person trying to manage two carts is always the same: "So, you have two carts."

Don't be *that person* the next time you see this happening. Come up with some new opening lines. I'm still noodling with these ideas, but so far I have:

- "Someone's getting all of the great bargains!"
- "Can you point me in the direction of the Doublemint gum?
- "Do you have any 2 for 1 coupons?"

I admit those lines are only slightly better than "So, you have two carts," but at least it's a start that will hopefully fuel your creativity. Make sure you use a TV Show Jerry voice when talking to The Amphibians.

SEINFELD FAN FUN

MOST LIKELY TO BE AN AMPHIBIAN
Kramer

LEAST LIKELY TO BE AN AMPHIBIAN
Frank Costanza

MOST LIKELY TO WORK FOR A COMPANY THAT
ENCOURAGES PEOPLE TO PUSH TWO CARTS AT ONCE
George

MOST LIKELY TO COMMENT ABOUT A PERSON
PUSHING TWO CARTS
Jerry

MOST LIKELY TO TRY AND USE THE CARTS TO
COLLECT BOTTLES AND CANS FOR DEPOSIT MONEY
Kramer and Newman

MOST LIKELY TO BE CONFUSED BY THE AMPHIBIANS
Lloyd Braun

CAUSE YOU CAN DONATE TO IF YOU'RE SELLING OLD
GROCERY CARTS FOR CHARITY

The Human Fund

REAL WORLD FUN

HAPPY HOUR DISCUSSION TOPICS

- Because our society likes to pit things against one another, I wonder whether Jerry Seinfeld's beloved Superman could handle more grocery carts than the Hulk.
- Besides Kramer, which *Seinfeld* character could handle the most baskets at once?
- Is it possible to handle three carts at once?
- Is it OK to tie the carts together, or would that be considered cheating?
- Of all the companies and imaginary companies featured on *Seinfeld*, which would be the most likely to sponsor an ad sign located on a grocery cart?

25

The Crop Dusters

Seinfeld mined humor from bad smells on several occasions, including the smell that Jerry could not get out of his car ("The Smelly Car," Season 4, Episode 20) and the smelly product George ordered from China to try and grow more hair ("The Tape," Season 3, Episode 8). The next item is sponsored by Beef-A-Reeno. Shout-out to Rusty the horse! ("The Rye," Season 7, Episode 11)

By now, you've probably heard the term "crop dusting." If not, it means something pretty simple. The Crop Dusters are people who pass gas in a public place, spreading a stinking mess, reminiscent of planes spraying farmers' crops with insecticides. Full confession: "The Crop Dusters" is a more elegant name than what I actually wrote in my diary, "The Grocery Store Smelly Farters."

I must say that some of the worst smells I have ever encountered have hit me like a brick wall while I was unsuspectingly pushing my grocery cart down the aisle. I'll leave the descriptions of some of those smells to your imagination.

I believe there are several different camps of Crop Dusters. The most sinister are the Intentional Crop Dusters. They practice premeditated crop dustings. They eat inordinate amounts of beans and broccoli before heading to the store. They look around to decide which person might be the most offended if they get dusted. They search for sections of the store where people gather in groups. On a perfect day, they can crop dust several register aisles as they quietly walk by. It's almost impossible to find the source of the crop dusting because you are temporarily debilitated when the smell hits you.

Almost as bad are The Sporting Crop Dusters. These folks are usually male, and they are typically teens and/or high school students. Underclass college students may also join in on the fun. They turn crop dusting into a grocery store sport by doing it over and over so many times that it becomes a game of tag for them. The Sporting Crop Dusters rate far lower on the Bad Smell Index. The noise of the dusting and the element of surprise are what makes the game such a fun sport for them.

There is humor to be mined from The Unintentional Crop Dusters. You may see the sweetest older lady, say hello, and then she is mortified because she is caught in this unintentional act. The worst ones are when a person apologizes to you before you realize you've been dusted.

Perhaps the most dangerous of the dusters is the group I call The Diaper Dusters. I'm a parent. My last name is Murphy. I know an extension of Murphy's Law states that dirty diapers often happen at the worst possible moment, in the worst possible place. That said, during my diary survey period, I wrote down the term "diaper bombs."

This happens when the mom or dad of the dirty diaper creator parks the cart with the epicenter of the crop dusting right next to you—and sometimes talks to their friend for a few minutes. The worst is if the diaper is stained or leaking, and you see it before the parent realizes it. If memory serves me right, I first used the term "diaper bombs" because someone changed their child's diaper and left the soiled one in a trash can inside the grocery store. The smell was so intense(ly bad) that several aisles were crop dusted. I felt bad for the young store employee who I saw getting tasked with changing out the trash bag.

One other diary note: One day I smelled something really bad in the air freshener aisle. I thought that was an unexpected place to get crop dusted. There were three of us in the aisle. An older lady in front of me suddenly got pretty mad. She grabbed a can of air freshener and sprayed it to freshen up the aisle. She made a mean face at both me and another lady who was just in front of the lady spraying the air freshener.

I promise, even though I am guilty of crop dusting once in a while, this time it was not me. I made a note in my diary that it would be funniest if the older lady spraying the can was actually the crop duster. The note also mentioned the taunt I learned in second grade: "The person that smelled it, dealt it."

I also spent several hours on Google doing research for you. These five quick facts are from Dr. Billy Goldberg and Mark Leyner.

- The average person passes gas 14 times a day.
- Women fart as much as men.
- People produce about half a liter of farts a day.
- Farts have been clocked at a speed of 10 feet per second.
- Less than 1% of a fart's constituents are what makes it stink.

SEINFELD FAN FUN

MOST LIKELY TO GET AWAY WITH CROP DUSTING
Elaine

LEAST LIKELY TO BE A CROP DUSTER
Jerry

LEAST LIKELY TO BE AFFECTED BY A CROP DUSTER
Kramer

MOST LIKELY TO TALK ABOUT A CROP DUSTER FOR
MONTHS AFTER BEING VICTIM TO ONE
George

MOST LIKELY TO FIND A BATHROOM WITH A FLUSH
LIKE A JET ENGINE WHILE CROP DUSTING
Kramer

MOST LIKELY TO LAND IN THE GUINNESS BOOK FOR
CROP DUSTING
Rusty The Horse

SECRETLY KNOWS A LOT MORE ABOUT CROP
DUSTING THAN YOU MIGHT THINK
Mr. Marbles

REAL WORLD FUN

Science Alert took a deep dive into smells in the 2018 article "These
Are The Worst Smells In The World, According to Science" by
Prajakta Dhapte. The article referenced a study in *The Journal of
Neuroscience* that said that bad smells can be boiled down to their
underlying molecular structure. The study focused on 1,500 proper-
ties of 150 different molecules in order to establish a relationship
between the pleasantness of a smell and the way its molecules are
arranged.

The research team from University of California, Berkeley,
found that molecular weight and electron density are closely associated with how we perceive the qualities of a scent. Heavier, more
spread-out molecules tend to be associated with bad smells, while
lighter, more compact molecules are more pleasant. These smell
experts believe that something even deeper could be at work—it's

not just what a chemical smells like, but how our brain responds to it that makes it awful.

All that said, here are the smells they picked as the worst in the world.

The Planet Uranus

Research says the planet smells like rotten eggs. This is due to the abundance of a gas called hydrogen sulfide in the atmosphere of Uranus.

The Durian Fruit

This notorious fruit can smell so bad that it once led to a massive evacuation at the University of Melbourne after students feared there was a gas leak. Turns out it was a rotten durian fruit, the smell of which carried over the university's air conditioning. The durian fruit gets its smell from 44 active odor compounds that can smell like anything from a rotten egg to delicious caramel.

The Stinking Corpse Lily (Rafflesia Arnoldii)

It is said to smell like a dead, decaying corpse, with a hint of fish and sweaty socks. Found in southeast Asia, it's the National Flower of Indonesia. In fact, it's the largest single flower in the world at one meter across. It ranks as the smelliest flower, right alongside the famed Titan Arum.

While the Titan Arum takes about a decade between flowerings, the Corpse Lily blossoms far more often, taking several months at a time, each blossom having a life span of 4–5 days. This foul-smelling flower is now on the verge of extinction and is a protected species.

Vieux Boulogne Cheese

The Vieux Boulogne is the smelliest cheese in the world. Some people describe it as smelling like a cow's rear.

Ancient Excrement

Smell now, smell later is the rule here. We're talking feces that still stink after 700 years. Archaeologists conducting an evacuation of a medieval latrine in the Danish city of Odense found that 14th century toilets, which were nothing but repurposed barrels, were still reeking of poop. That's serious staying power for a stink.

The Lesser Anteater

Don't be swayed by its cute face, because the Lesser Anteater is 5–7 times smellier than a skunk. But like the skunk, it uses its stench to ward off any unwanted visitors and predators.

26

The Kissy Faces

*E*arlier, we talked about the Grocery Store Schmoopies and discussed pet names. Despite their silly voices and sometimes hilarious nicknames, they are usually less obnoxious than the group outlined in this next diary entry. This next bunch is made up of people who are comfortable making out in public places. It reminds me of "The Raincoats" episode of *Seinfeld* when Jerry makes out at the movies. This was a two-part episode during the fifth season—for completists, the 82nd and 83rd episodes, or Episodes 18 and 19, Season 5. Yes, the movie (where the aforementioned making out happened) was "Schindler's List."

PDA. TMI. OMG.

I'm talking about The Kissy Faces, people who make out in the grocery store. You're trying to grab some Cocoa Puffs, and they are all over each other, going cuckoo about something else entirely. Kissy faces look great as emojis, but they're distracting—and sometimes downright gross in real life.

The next time you go to the grocery store, however, you need to realize you are frequenting the new singles hotspot. It's true. The Takeout says supermarkets are the new singles hotspot.

What's more, The Wall Street Journal says meeting people while shopping is low-key, non-confrontational, and doesn't involve deviating from your normal routine.

The Takeout even details the rise of groceraunts—supermarkets with restaurants, wine bars, coffee shops, and other dining options. This is a move by grocery stores to encourage more people to hang out longer in-store and treat the supermarket as a social gathering place. And unlike clubs or online dating platforms, the grocery store is a place where people feel comfortable.

I sincerely can't believe *The Bachelor* or *The Bachelorette* have not staged a season in the supermarket. Looking for Mr. or Miss Right? They might just come walking by as you are deciding what items to buy at the grocery store.

Alright, Supermarket Romeos and Juliets, NBC's *The Today Show* offers seven tips for finding love when grocery shopping. Most of them would make great *Seinfeld* material.

1. Choose the Right Department:
Psychologist Antonia Hall says the produce aisle, meat department, deli, and checkout line are the most ideal places for starting conversations with strangers.

2. Be Approachable: Hall says not to put pressure on yourself to leave with a date, or even a phone number. She says eye contact and smiles make for great initial connections. She says to be approachable and presentable. Have a positive attitude and a smile.

3. Put Your Phone Away: One of the main reasons people have a hard time connecting in real life is because they are obsessed with their cyber social life. Put your phone away. Take in your surroundings. Smile. Make eye contact.

4. Be Attentive To Detail: Check people's hands for wedding bands. You can learn a lot from a person's basket. It's usually obvious if they are cooking for one, or for a whole family. Frozen dinners, single steak packages, and small portions are telltale signs of single people. If you see family packs of items and large quantities of meat, the chances of them being taken are greater.

5. Keep Cool: Don't look nervous or uncomfortable. Try to be easy-going and friendly. Talk to people as you see them. Don't stand too long next to someone, or they might start to feel uncomfortable. Look for opportunities, summon your courage, step in, and say hello.

6. Start a Conversation:

You can start by acknowledging what they are looking at, then ask a question about it. For example, if a person is looking at a vegetable, you could say, "I cook for myself almost every night, and while I'm great at steak, vegetables are my weakness. How are you planning on preparing that broccoli?" When you ask someone questions, and they give you advice or information, they are investing in you, and they automatically feel more connected to you. Try to expand the conversation beyond vegetables. You might follow up by asking their favorite food, what wine goes best with it, or where they like to go out to eat when they are not cooking.

7. Seal The Deal:

Once contact is established, and you've chatted for a few minutes, it's time to take it to the next level and invite them out. Tell them you enjoyed talking to them and set up the next conversation by offering your phone number, or asking for theirs. Something as innocuous as "Would you like to grab coffee sometime?" might work.

. . .

SEINFELD FAN FUN

MOST LIKELY TO BE A GROCERY STORE ROMEO & JULIET
Jerry (*I mean… not even Schindler's List is off limits!*)

MOST LIKELY TO BREAK UP AFTER GROCERY STORE ROMEO AND JULIET ACTIVITY
Elaine and Puddy

MOST LIKELY TO SHOOT VIDEOS OF ROMEOS AND JULIETS
Kramer

MOST LIKELY TO TRY AND PICK UP SOMEONE IN THE STORE BY ASKING THEM TO PLAY FROLF
George

MOST LIKELY TO FIND SOMETHING SPECTACULAR IN THE STORE
Teri Hatcher

REAL WORLD FUN

MORE INFORMATION

- I would add "Don't talk to Larry King" in a grocery store to *The Today's Show's* list. King recently filed for his 7th divorce.
- Elizabeth Taylor had eight marriages to seven husbands. She married Richard Burton twice.
- Glynn Wolfe (1908–1997) was a Baptist minister who was famous for holding the record for the largest number

of monogamous marriages—29! His shortest marriage lasted 19 days, and his longest lasted 11 years. Three of his marriages were to a woman he had previously divorced. Wolfe's final marriage was to Linda Wolfe, who holds the record for the most-married woman, at 23 times. Glynn Wolfe had approximately 40 children. Sadly, when he died, none of the 29 women he legally married, and only one of his children, attended the funeral service.

- In the same Army commissary that I referenced in the earlier "Fifi Story," there was a ninth grade Kissy Face Incident. My buddy and his girlfriend thought it would be funny to see how long they could kiss in the store before an adult said something to them. They got the great job in the game of playing the role of the kissers. Me? I had to be the timekeeper. We all waited for somebody to walk down the aisle. As a lady did so, they started kissing. I acted like I wasn't with them and was perusing the shelves for potato chips. I counted 10 seconds, then 15, 30, and 60 seconds. They were running out of breath by now, but the lady was not paying much attention.

- My buddy considered himself a legend for coming up with this game. He played "The Kissing Game" with two other girls during the course of that school year. All three times he made it to the full 60 seconds without being interrupted by an adult. I lost track of him after that year. I still search Google and Facebook to see if I can find this kissing legend. You might have guessed that I was so impressed with his game because I was way too scared to try and kiss a girl when I was this age. Please don't e-mail me to ask how old I was when I first kissed a girl.

27

The Clear Cuppers

*S*ome of us have an optimistic outlook on life and can be described as glass-half-full people. These folks always think good things will happen. Other people see life more pessimistically, so they are said to be glass-half-empty people. Then there are The Clear Cuppers. They don't pay for the glass, but they sure enjoy drinking out of it.

The Clear Cuppers hang out at almost any place where beverages are available for purchase. I just happened to spot the latest one in my local grocery store. They take more advantage of a situation than actor Jon Lovitz guest-starring in a *Seinfeld* episode ("The Scofflaw," Season 6, Episode 13).

Here's how it works. To ensure proper beverage diplomacy, most stores and restaurants offer you a clear cup if you are ordering water instead of purchasing a beverage from their soda fountain. This often happens in bars as well.

The Clear Cuppers see this as a major opportunity. They pocket the savings, look around so as not to be noticed, and then they use the clear cup to get soda, tea, lemonade, what have you, instead of water. They almost always smirk right after filling the clear cup, as if they are laughing to themselves that they have beaten the game—and saved money in the process.

For whatever reason, people who notice a Clear Cupper going about their shenanigans usually do not make a fuss. I've never seen anyone challenge The Clear Cupper or report them to the restaurant. Is this such a petty activity that it registers just below the threshold of what the average person considers a serious crime?

I'd love to hear what the police have to say about this activity, but I'm scared to ask the police officers I know about it. It seems like such a silly thing to ask about when they deal with murderers, rapists, kidnappers, bank robbers, etc.

I'm thinking that if you do tell the restaurant manager—especially a fast food restaurant manager—about The Clear Cupper, they might just point at the person and give out a half-hearted "Hey, you need to pay for that drink next time" warning.

Maybe the best thing you can do to discourage Clear Cuppers is to call them by name. Use an authoritative voice, walk up to them and say, "I saw what you did there, Clear Cupper." Use a TV Show Jerry serious voice while doing so, and don't forget to point at them. Somehow, I think getting called a Clear Cupper is worse than getting caught clear cupping. It makes me feel bad just thinking about somebody calling me a Clear Cupper.

A close cousin to The Clear Cupper is The Cup Re-User. This is a person who brings in a cup to a fast food restaurant, one that they have previously used at that restaurant, or another location of that same restaurant—and fills it again (usually with little or no shame).

Convenience stores started this nonsense with their ginormous refillable cups the size of industrial trash cans. Now, people think they can just keep their cups and fill them up everywhere. We once saw a family with a car full of cups for various places. Obviously, they are not ashamed to "go in for the free refill." As Frank Costanza says, "Serenity now!"

SEINFELD FAN FUN

MOST LIKELY TO BE A CLEAR CUPPER
It's a tie between George and Frank Costanza

MOST LIKELY TO SPOT A CLEAR CUPPER
Elaine

MOST LIKELY TO HANG OUT WITH CLEAR CUPPERS
Kramer

MOST LIKELY TO FORM A SINISTER PARTNERSHIP WITH CLEAR CUPPERS
Newman

MOST LIKELY TO GET A GREAT COMEDY BIT FROM WATCHING CLEAR CUPPERS
Kenny Bania… just kidding, it's Jerry.

MOST LIKELY TO BE TAKEN IN BY CLEAR CUPPERS AND INSTALLED IN A PUPPET REGIME
Kramer

REAL WORLD FUN

MORE INFORMATION

- Fact Retriever reports that McDonald's sells more than 1 billion cups of coffee each year around the world. McDonald's sells 500 million cups a day in the U.S. alone.
- What is the best McDonald's location for The Clear Cuppers to not be noticed? That may be in Hong Kong

because the top 10 busiest McDonald's restaurants are all there.

- Famous weather person Willard Scott was the first Ronald McDonald.
- Famous people who say they worked at McDonald's include Sharon Stone, Shania Twain, Jay Leno, Rachel McAdams and Pink.

28

The Cookie Monsters

*L*et me start by saying that one of my greatest guilty pleasures in life is chomping down on a whole sleeve of Thin Mint Girl Scout cookies that's been perfectly chilled in the refrigerator for at least 24 hours. Earlier, we have talked about life, liberty, and all that jazz. Properly chilled Thin Mints are as important as all of those for me.

Okay, I wanted to assert this first before venturing into the Girl Scout semi-criticism waters. That way you know I mean it when I say, "I strongly support Girl Scouts, especially their civic activities and their cookie-selling efforts."

You understand that I like and wholeheartedly support Girl Scouts, right?

That said, when The Cookie Monsters come out, you better keep your head on a swivel and watch out. No GPS is needed to find The Cookie Monsters. Unlike the Keebler Elves who live in trees, The Cookie Monsters are everywhere.

Each year, the Girl Scouts have thousands of kids trying to sell cookies. Most of them live on my street. You don't have to mark your calendar for cookie season. You'll hear about it. Again. And again. And again. And again. And a fifth again.

It now seems that every troop from every nook and cranny of the city gets a chance to sell you a box of cookies at every store you visit. I saw several vans pull up in front of one of my grocery stores this past season. I had my diary ready. Dozens of girls paced the front of the store like hot dog and beer vendors at a baseball game. Their logic is impeccable. We're hungry. We need things from the store. Why can't one of those things be Girl Scout cookies?

At the time, I had already purchased six boxes of Thin Mints over several weeks. This renegade troop rolled their eyes, shrugged their shoulders, and acted like I was Adolf Hitler for trying to say no to them. To try and diffuse the situation, I gave one girl a donation of a dollar bill because getting by her meant I had a clear shot to my car. She was confused and started telling people that I hadn't given her enough money. I had to explain to an angry Girl Scout mom that I had made a donation because I already had six boxes at home. Most days, I'd rather talk to the police than to an angry Girl Scout mom. You know what she said? "We take credit cards. You need to purchase a couple more boxes from us, because they are great gifts for anybody at any time of the year."

I underlined "did not purchase on this day" in my diary.

Later that same week, I was subjected to another hard sell as I tried to get into the drugstore. I broke out the six-boxes story to this troop, and they said I needed to buy another type of cookie because they could win a trip to Cabo if they met their goal. "Cookies Over Cabo" is the working title of the story I'm developing about that experience. I may need another box of Thin Mints and at least 24 hours of refrigeration time to help me write that story.

SEINFELD FAN FUN

MOST LIKELY TO BE RED-FACE ANNOYED BY "GIRL SCOUT NAZIS"
George

MOST LIKELY TO BE BOTHERED MORE THAN ONCE BY THE COOKIE MONSTERS
Jerry

LEAST LIKELY TO ENJOY GIRL SCOUT HUMOR
Susie (Elaine)

MOST LIKELY TO TRY AND TRADE GIRL SCOUT COOKIES FOR CUBAN CIGARS
Kramer

MOST LIKELY TO HAVE SOLD THE MOST GIRL SCOUT COOKIES BACK IN THE DAY
Sue Ellen Mischke

MOST LIKELY TO TRY AND IMPRESS GIRL SCOUT MOMS BY ADOPTING A STRETCH OF HIGHWAY
Kramer

REAL WORLD FUN

- Google says that we've bought as much as 785 million dollars of Girl Scout cookies in a single year.
- Statistic Brain says 2.75 million girl scouts sell these cookies, which come in up to 28 different varieties.
- According to Business Insider, these are the five top-selling types of Girl Scout cookies:

- 5. Shortbread (Trefoils)
- 4. Peanut Butter Sandwiches (Do-si-dos)
- 3. Peanut Butter Patties (Tagalongs)
- 2. Samoas (Caramel deLites)
- 1. Thin Mints

- It's interesting to follow up on the national ranking with a listing of the most popular Girl Scout cookies in each state. This information is courtesy of Insider.

Thin Mints are the most popular Girl Scout Cookie in almost half the states in our country:

Arkansas
Arizona
California
Delaware
Hawaii
Idaho
Illinois
Indiana
Maryland
Michigan
Minnesota
Nebraska
New Hampshire
Nevada
Ohio
Oklahoma
Oregon
Rhode Island
South Dakota
Tennessee
Utah
Virginia
West Virginia

Samoas reign supreme in 18 states:

Colorado
Florida
Georgia

Iowa
Kansas
Kentucky
Louisiana
Massachusetts
Maine
Missouri
North Carolina
North Dakota
New Jersey
New Mexico
New York
Pennsylvania
Texas
Washington

Tagalongs are the favorite in six states, plus the District of Columbia:

Alabama
Connecticut
Washington D.C.
Mississippi
Montana
South Carolina
Wisconsin

Do-si-dos top the list in two states:

Vermont
Wyoming

Thin Mints are my favorite, but they were not listed as the favorite in the state where I live, Texas. What happened, y'all?

29

The Teachable Moments

I'm the father of teenage boys. I've coached teenage boys. I've been a teenage boy. I know that teenagers sometimes don't give their 100% when they work. I think it all starts when you ask them to do things like take out the trash and empty the dishwasher. Invariably, the empty trash can in the kitchen gets left without a new trash bag. In addition, the silverware is often left behind in what is proclaimed to be an empty dishwasher. These are teachable moments that seem to play out again and again. I was once the student for these lessons, and now I'm the teacher.

In my diary, I noticed this type of behavior carrying over into certain areas of the grocery store. I'm sorry to blame teenage employees for these teachable moments, but I'm trying to tell myself that grownups wouldn't do these types of things. Yes, I know that is a ridiculous idea.

Here are two levels of The Teachable Moments.

LEVEL 1: EASY TEACHABLE MOMENT

. . .

BAGGERS GONE WILD

Normally, the baggers—most of them teenagers—do a pretty decent job at my favorite stores. Just before Christmas, however, someone who had probably skipped bagger training gave my groceries the Freddy Krueger treatment. It was a nightmare on any street.

Six words. Frozen turkey on top of eggs. Only half of them survived—and you can't switch out broken ones once you leave the store. It also made thawing the big bird its own special nightmare. You just can't wipe off all of the egg. It gets smeared everywhere. Even paper towel companies shy away from these types of messes.

The nightmare didn't end there. Canned goods had been placed on top of one bag such that they smashed my bread into an almost unrecognizable heap. Poor little loaf. I had to laugh because it looked so ridiculous.

Because I've watched *Seinfeld* so much, I started saying "Newman" in a TV Show Jerry voice each time I discovered another challenge with my grocery bags. After the first couple of disasters, I started hoping for more because it was all so bizarre.

My Bagger Gone Wild did not disappoint me.

Cold items were mixed with my bathroom cleaning products. A box of ant traps was on top of my package of hamburger.

In reality, the whole shopping trip would have been better if my bagger had just stood there and done nothing. I chalked up the whole incident to the store needing extra employees for the holidays and not having enough time to train them. Or, my Bagger Gone Wild was not supposed to be working that day and was pretty peeved that he'd been called in to work.

This is Level One of The Teachable Moments. Proper training can easily correct such indifference, although I did not complain. If I can't get my trash can and dishwasher projects under control, what right do I have to complain about one rogue bagger?

. . .

LEVEL 2: ADVANCED TEACHABLE MOMENT

FLOOR DECAL FAILS

Yes, I'm pretty picky about where they put the stick-to-the-floor decal ads for my Tony the Tiger cereal. Some varieties are called floor clings. Yes, I've googled floor decals. I'm also picky about how flat store employees get the decal when they place it on the floor.

At my store, the decal was wrinkled, and Tony's left ear was almost touching his right ear. This was not grrrrrreat. Does anybody check this work? I can still feel the frustration as I read my diary entry from that day.

Why would they put the wrinkled decal on the opposite side of the aisle next to the Pop Tarts? Were there no Milton the Toaster floor decal ads for Pop Tarts? Tony the Tiger would not have been pleased. The voice of Tony the Tiger would also not have been pleased.

What's more, in addition to the floor decal being misplaced by the Pop Tarts, why is the Tony the Tiger floor decal at the far end of the aisle, way past where the Frosted Flakes cereal lives?

My wife thinks it's ridiculous that I even pointed out this "floor decal fail" and considered talking about it to somebody at the store. I wanted to go into my best George Costanza stance and say, "I couldn't help but notice there are some challenges with the Tony the Tiger floor decal."

My wife talked me out of my Costanza-flavored cereal rant. I stayed quiet. Per usual, she was right.

The next week, however, the Tony the Tiger floor decal was gone. I'm guessing that the wrinkled decal tripped somebody and/or got gobbled up in somebody's grocery cart wheels.

For fun, I had to do some extra research. Statista reported that 8.78 million Americans consumed 10 portions or more of Frosted Flakes in a seven-day survey period in 2019. You get 8 million Americans doing anything, and it's certainly a Level 2 Teachable

Moment. Another take-away from here is the fact that millions of Americans care about Tony the Tiger and Frosted Flakes. So the least we can do is get the floor decal project under control.

Later that month, I saw the same floor decal, correctly placed right in front of the Frosted Flakes display at Walmart. And because my Seinfeld Eyes needed to see it, I checked on the decal at Walmart again about six weeks later. It was still there. They had mastered the Advanced Teachable Moment level.

George Costanza would be proud of me.

SEINFELD FAN FUN

CHARACTER MOST LIKELY TO BAG YOUR GROCERIES BADLY
Newman

CHARACTER MOST LIKELY TO ARGUE ABOUT TONY THE TIGER DECALS
George

CHARACTER MOST LIKELY TO SABOTAGE A FLOOR DECAL PROJECT FOR PERSONAL GAIN
Elaine

CHARACTER MOST LIKELY TO WEAR A TONY THE TIGER MASCOT COSTUME
Kramer

PERSON MOST LIKELY TO PERFORM A FUNNY MASCOT VOICE
Larry David

CHARACTER MOST LIKELY TO DESTROY A DECAL OF JERRY IF HE SEES ONE IN THE STORE
Newman

REAL WORLD FUN

The Ten Random Facts website shared some interesting facts about stickers from *The History of Stickers* and *Sticker Printing Facts*:

- Stickers have their origins in revenue or tax stamps, which were used as early as the mid-1700s.
- The first adhesive postage stamps in the world were used in the UK in 1840.
- The first modern stickers, known as self-adhesive labels, with a peel-off backing, were made in 1935 by R. Stanton Avery from Oklahoma, who founded the Avery company.
- It is believed that bumper stickers were first made by Forest Gill, who was a printer, to advertise Rocky Mountain's Rock City attraction.
- Stickers can be sparkly, smelly (scratch and sniff), 3D, fabric, acrylic, or plain.

30

The Grocery Store Mary Tyler Moores

*M*y Seinfeld Eyes tend to zero in on quirky things. But after logging crazy item after crazy item, I wrote in my diary that I needed to try and focus my Seinfeld Eyes on something happy or cheerful that I saw in the grocery store. I think I had just watched "The Sponge" (Season 7, Episode 9) and been inspired by the goodness of Jerry's girlfriend Lena. Don't worry, there was no hugging and probably no learning. What I noticed were the Grocery Store Mary Tyler Moores.

If you've never seen an episode of the sitcom *Mary Tyler Moore*, please watch one soon. It is a pretty impressive sitcom that inspired Jerry Seinfeld himself. At the very least, check out the theme song on Amazon Music, iTunes, or the like. It's happy, optimistic, inspiring, and goes as follows:

Who can turn the world on with her smile?
Who can take a nothing day, and suddenly make it all seem worthwhile?
Well, it's you girl, and you should know it.
With each glance and every little movement you show it.
Love is all around, no need to waste it
You can never tell, why don't you take it.

You're gonna make it after all.
You're gonna make it after all.

Make sure you also check out Joan Jett's version of the "Love Is All Around" *Mary Tyler Moore* theme. There is a really badass YouTube clip of her perfuming the song on Letterman. Seeing a video of one of my favorite '80s icons paying tribute to a beloved '70s icon still brings tears to my eyes.

Descriptions of the Mary Richards character say she was iconic but fallible, competent but flappable. Mary was human and strong enough to laugh with and be laughed at. In 1999, Entertainment Weekly ranked her hat toss in the opening credits as television's second greatest moment. Moore once described the moment as an expression of "freedom, exuberance, spontaneity and joy—all in one gesture."

If you focus your Seinfeld Eyes correctly, you can see positive people in the grocery store who try and do their part to improve the human condition. I call them Grocery Store Mary Tyler Moores.

GSMTMs put a lot of effort into a grocery store trip. They are usually dressed a little more nicely and act a little more friendly than the rest of the people in the store. It's the sincerity of their friendliness that matters the most. When these folks say, "Have a nice day," they really mean it. When they say your shirt looks nice, they really mean it. They are not affiliated with the store, but they are not just shopping—they are helping with everything.

While compiling my diary, I saw GSMTMs text a family queso recipe to a person they just met. I saw GSMTMs picking up some random trash in the store. I saw GSMTMs complimenting people whose pink hair seemed crazy to me. I saw GSMTMs helping the person cooking food samples. Little things can mean a lot. Watch for the sincere, kind demeanor of the GSMTM. It can warm your day —and maybe change your life.

The GSMTM who complimented the pink hair was my wife, Jenny. She's also the GSMTM who helped all of those Shelf Climbers.

Thank you, Jenny. You're the perfect complement to a person who sees the grocery store (and the world) through Seinfeld Eyes.

SEINFELD FAN FUN

CHARACTER MOST LIKELY TO THINK THE GROCERY STORE MARY TYLER MOORE LOOKS LIKE MARISA TOMEI
George

CHARACTER MOST LIKELY TO THINK THEY ARE A GROCERY STORE MARY TYLER MOORE
Elaine

CHARACTER MOST LIKELY TO SPOT A GROCERY STORE MARY TYLER MOORE
Kramer

CHARACTER MOST LIKELY TO HAVE ALTERED THE SIZE TAG ON HIS JEANS BEFORE TALKING TO A GROCERY STORE MARY TYLER MOORE
Jerry

CHARACTER MOST LIKELY TO DATE A GROCERY STORE MARY TYLER MOORE AND THEN BREAK UP WITH HER BECAUSE SHE'S TOO GOOD
Jerry

REAL WORLD FUN

- *The Mary Tyler Moore Show* is an American sitcom starring Mary Tyler Moore; it originally aired on CBS from 1970 to 1977. It won 29 Primetime Emmy Awards.

- The show launched three spin-offs: *Rhoda*, *Phyllis*, and *Lou Grant*.
- The Writers Guild of America ranked The Mary Tyler Moore Show number six on its list of the "101 Best Written TV Series of All Time."
- In the fall of 1992, Nick at Nite began broadcasting the series nightly, launching it with a week-long "Mary-thon," and it became the network's top-rated series.
- In her book "Seinfeldia," author Jennifer Armstrong reports that Jerry Seinfeld and other New York comedians frequently watched *The Mary Tyler Moore* show, because they could see the re-runs of the show late at night after doing comedy sets. In interviews, the comedians would often describe, in vivid detail, their crushes on Mary Richards.
- Sonny Curtis sang the show's theme song. He played on some of Buddy Holly's early sessions. In 1955 and 1956 he opened concerts for Elvis Presley. He wrote the popular song "I Fought The Law." In 2012, Curtis was inducted into the Rock and Roll Hall of Fame as a member of the Crickets (Buddy Holly's band).

Sponsor

This book is made possible in part by the good folks at Jiffy Park. Choose Jiffy Park for all of your parking and companionship needs.

Thank you.

Part III—The List

The Seinfeld Fan Grocery List

*T*he next time you head out to the grocery store, make a Seinfeld Fan List of items to buy. Here are 30 suggestions for you.

30 ITEMS SEINFELD FANS SHOULD CONSIDER PUTTING ON THEIR GROCERY LIST

- A Block of Cheese the Size of a Car Battery
- Bear Claws
- Beef-A-Reeno
- Bosco Chocolate Syrup
- Cereal (About 10 Boxes)
- Cider (Tart)
- Drake's Coffee Cake
- Fancy Astronaut Pens
- Food (For Lovemaking)
- Fusilli

- Glamour Magazine
- Hennigan's
- Instant Coffee
- Junior Mints
- Knives and Forks (For Candy Bar)
- Mackinaw Peaches
- Marble Rye
- Muffins
- Mutton
- Non-Fat Yogurt
- Oh Henry! Candy Bar
- Ovaltine
- Pepsi and Ring Dings (For Party)
- Pez (Get New Dispenser)
- Salad (Big)
- Soft-Boiled Egg (For A Quickie)
- Today's Sponge (Case)
- Tyler Chicken
- Vegetable Lasagna
- Yoo-Hoo

SHOPPING REMINDERS

- All starches are scams.
- Don't talk to your food.
- Chocolate Babka > Cinnamon Babka
- Gandhi loved Triscuits.
- Do not buy gum—You don't want to be "The Gum Guy."

Part IV—The Games

HOW YOU CAN SEINFELD THE STORE

Seinfeld's mixing of fiction with real life gave us crazy characters that were allowed to push the envelope much further than most of us can in real life.

The motivation from their great game of "What if..." coupled with my love of grocery store frivolity and game shows gave rise to many ideas for grocery store games while I compiled the diary.

(CUE THE GAME SHOW MUSIC)

It's time to celebrate 30 years of *Seinfeld* by using *Seinfeld* as a verb and listing some ways in which you can *Seinfeld* the store.

Disclaimer: These are silly ideas for games that you should never try in the grocery store or anywhere else. You should probably stop reading this section and skip to the next chapter.

I knew you'd keep reading. Anyway, for the sake of humanity, I stopped short of giving you 30 games you can play in the grocery store to help celebrate 30 years of *Seinfeld*. Instead, here's a six-pack. It seems appropriate that it should be a six-pack when discussing over-the-top, silly, goofy grocery store games.

Second Disclaimer: Again, please skip the rest of this section and go to the next part.

1

The Abraham Lincoln Game

*Y*ou were warned—twice.

These days, people are sporting many different styles of beards. There are scruffy beards, long beards, beards that are dyed different colors, and so on. Watching them through Seinfeld Eyes, I have theorized that Abraham Lincoln popularized the beard movement. In fact, a lot of today's bearded wonders may be riding Honest Abe's coattails.

Much of this beard love is fueled by those "No Shave November" folks. Not even Jerry's regular barber, Enzo ("The Barber," Season 5, Episode 8) could derail this movement. Both of my sons are part of the NSN movement. I'm sure I would have jumped headlong into NSN when I was their age. Some of those NSN folks can look pretty silly, but my Seinfeld Eyes usually can't look away. Remember, the NSN movement started to help raise cancer awareness. Please do whatever you can to help fight cancer. That said, let's add to the grocery store fun.

Now, I play the "Abraham Lincoln Game" in the grocery store. It's the most fun to play this game 4–5 days into November when NSN is getting into full swing. It's truly an easy game to learn, plus it helps sharpen your love of history. No worries if you didn't pay attention in history class; just focus your Seinfeld Eyes on the facial hair.

All you need to do is watch people in the store and find the ones with beards. Next, find your Rail-Splitter (another nickname for President Lincoln). In short, you need to decide which one would be the most likely to play the role of Lincoln if Steven Spielberg called and asked you to cast that role in his next movie.

Of course, you can't let Steve Spielberg down. It's up to you to decide if the person needs to be as tall as Lincoln, look somewhat like the 16th President, fill the shoes of the Great Emancipator, etc. Sometimes, I'll travel back all the way across the store to view a Lincoln Game finalist one more time. You can't just hand out hypothetical ranking privileges to anybody. If, on glimpsing a finalist, I feel like I've entered a time warp, and we are somewhere near Gettysburg, I know I have a winner.

The criteria you use, and the way you play the game is up to you. Maybe your Lincoln Game winner is short, has a goatee instead of a beard, is not white, is not male, or lots of other possibilities. They're your Seinfeld Eyes. Take a good look!

Recommended Do's and Don'ts of the Abraham Lincoln Game:

DO

- Say "Four score…" to see if you can get a reaction from a person who is a finalist in the Abraham Lincoln Game.
- Ask an Abraham Lincoln Game finalist if they enjoy reading books.
- Ask a finalist if they know any women named Mary Todd Lincoln.
- Take pictures of winners (with their permission) and post them on the Fun Stories Facebook and Twitter sites.

DON'T

- Go all Crazy Joe Davola with the game and utter the phrase, "Sic semper tyrannis" while scoping out potential winners. That's crossing the line from fun into something more twisted.
- Ask a finalist if they like to wear a hat when they go to the theater.
- Ask people if they will read your grocery list in their best Abraham Lincoln voice.

2

The Fake Announcement Game

*E*arlier we talked about people in the store trying to sound hip when they make announcements. This type of announcement is different than that one. The Fake Announcement Game is where you take it upon yourself to imitate the store's PA system in order to make your own announcements in the store. How loud is your voice? Can you get people in your aisle to think it is coming from the grocery store's PA system?

In sixth grade, this classmate of mine named Kevin could imitate the voice of the lady who worked in the office. That lady would frequently come over the intercom to talk to the teachers. He'd wait until this one teacher started writing on the chalkboard and had his back turned.

He'd first imitate the little beep the intercom made, and then imitate the office lady's voice saying, "Mr. Teacher." Of course, he used the teacher's real name. When the teacher turned to listen, the intercom would suddenly go quiet. The teacher would eventually start writing on the board again.

Soon, the fake intercom noise would happen again, and the voice would say again, "Mr. Teacher." After two or three more instances of this, our teacher would walk down to the office to tell them the intercom was malfunctioning. One day, a repair man showed up, pulled out the speaker box, and rewired it. We were chuckling the whole time, and Mr. Teacher had to tell us to settle down.

Kevin fooled "Mr. Teacher" three different times that sixth grade year. As an added bonus, he fooled two substitute teachers and a guest speaker. We'd make him do "The Speaker Voice" over and over during kickball games on the playground. He was a sixth grade celebrity. He really should have gone into show business.

If you have this type of talent, be careful with it. Remember that "great power, great responsibility" stuff from *Spider-Man*. Don't be too crazy and say there's a hurricane on the way or a lot of free stuff being handed out somewhere. Just say, "Attention shoppers, this is important…" and then stop. People will stop in their tracks and keep listening. Then use your Seinfeld Eyes to come up with something fun, but not dangerous. I would personally like to reward Make-Believe Mary with a surprise birthday serenade from all of the shoppers, but it probably wouldn't phase her.

On a final note, the fun is in creating your own message. Don't just step up and start blurting weird things into the store's real PA system. That's not funny, and it might get you arrested.

3

The Grocery Store Password Game

*T*his one is easy to play. You come up with a password. For example, the word "opossum." You then have to get somebody in the store to say your password out loud. To keep the game brief, I consider it a tennis match, where each time a person says something counts as hitting the ball. You need to get a random shopper to say the password in five responses (that is, in five hits of the ball) or less.

The crazier the word, the more points you should assign to it. I like to give points on a 1–10 scale with 1 being an easy word and 10 being a very difficult word. If you slip up and say the password before the person you are quizzing says it, you lose the game.

Here's how a recent game played out at the store.

PASSWORD: Opossum.

I assigned it 7 points. That's just the way I felt that day. There was no scientific research, or really any thought about it at all.

. . .

GOAL: **Get a random shopper to say the word within five responses in the conversation.**

ME: Wow, they have lots of sales because it's Back-To-School time.

RANDOM LADY: Do you have the app? There are even more sales.

ME: I tried to download the app, but it just lay there on my phone like one of those animals that likes to play dead. Do you know what I'm talking about?

RANDOM LADY: Yes, my phone is old too.

ME: We had one of those animals in our backyard the other day.

RANDOM LADY: Well, check out the app and see if you can get it to work.

ME: It's driving me crazy; I just can't remember the name of the things that play dead in the backyard.

RANDOM LADY: Groundhogs?

ME: (KNOWING HER NEXT RESPONSE WILL BE #5) No, I think it rhymes with awesome.

· · ·

RANDOM LADY: This is getting weird; you have a nice day.

ME: Yada, yada, yada—you can't win them all.

RANDOM LADY: I never much liked that *Seinfield* show.

ME: Opossum. The password was opossum. You know, the prehensile-tailed marsupial. I was trying to help you win a grocery store game.

RANDOM LADY: Are you with the store?

ME: I am today.

RANDOM LADY: Was there a prize?

ME: A gift certificate from Jiffy Park.

RANDOM LADY: I prefer cash prizes.

GAME VARIATIONS

THE CHECKOUT EDITION

In this game, you receive double points if you can get your checkout person to say the password before they draw up the total for your groceries. Of course, if you slip up and say the password before the person you are quizzing says it, you lose the game.

THE WORD LIST EDITION

This one has multiple players. It plays out like a scavenger hunt. All of the players go into the store with the same list of words. I recommend no more than five words. Three words might work even better. Each person has to collect all of the words on the list. They are out if they say a word, or if they fail to collect one of the words. For additional fun, players might have to collect all of the words while pushing a shopping cart, and then they must be the first person to return the cart to a predetermined location to be declared the winner.

4

The Show-Me-
The-Sample Game

While I refrained from creating The Crop Dusting Game, I did create The Show-Me-The-Sample Game. This is probably the most juvenile game you can play in the grocery store. Please don't terrorize unknown people with it. Play the game with a friend, a sibling, or your significant other.

As you may know, the weekend is the best time to get the most samples at the grocery store. It's all the fun you can mount on a toothpick!

It's best when only you know that the game is being played. The element of surprise is crucial. Look for a good time to temporarily separate yourself from the other person who will be in the game.

Seek out whatever you think is the messiest sample the store is handing out. Get two of them. Chew the samples thoroughly enough to create a mushy mess inside your mouth.

Find your friend.

Without letting anybody else see it—open your mouth, stick out your tongue, and show your friend the sample! Warning: If a nearby shopper sees your sloppy sample, you are disqualified.

After swallowing it, ask your friend to guess what type of food sample you have just shown them. If they guess correctly, the game is over. If they can't guess it, they must then get their own sample and show it to you. It must be a different type of food sample than the one you showed them.

SPECIAL NOTE:

It's fun before, during, and after the game to say enthusiastically (in a Cuba Gooding, Jr. "Show me the money" type of voice), "Show me the sample!"

YET ANOTHER DISCLAIMER:

I've never heard of a person being elected President or being chosen for the Supreme Court after playing this game.

5

The Winning-Both-Showcases Game

*T*urning to a far more sensible grocery store opportunity, this one is a guessing game. It mimics *The Price Is Right*. I call it The Winning-Both-Showcases Game.

Without using a calculator, try to guess the total cost of your groceries before the cashier starts ringing them up. By my rules, you need at least 16 items. That means you have a cart, and you are not in the 15 Items-or-Less Line. Anybody with reasonable math skills can guess the price of a pack of gum and a couple of food items.

On *The Price Is Right*, you must guess the cost of your showcase within $100 to win both showcases. In this game, you must guess the total cost of your groceries within $5. On *The Price Is Right*, you lose if you go over on your guess. Through Seinfeld Eyes, if you can guess within $5 over or under the total price, you are still a winner. Your prize for winning this game is grocery store pride. Everybody needs more of that.

I know some of you are saying, "But Scott, it's too much work to try and guess the cost of everything in my basket and get within $5 of the actual total." In that case, you can play the simplified version of The Winning-Both-Showcases Game.

In that game, you simply guess whether your groceries will cost over or under $100. If you have a ton of groceries, you might make the final over/under price $150 or $200. The main goal of all this activity is to *Seinfeld* the store and create more fun.

6

The Super Terrific Happy Battle Creek Extravaganza Game

*T*V Show Jerry (and Real Jerry) love to eat cereal. In the *Seinfeld* episode "The Checks" (Season 8, Episode 7), Jerry received hundreds of twelve-cent royalty checks from his appearance on the Japanese TV show, "Super Terrific Happy Hour." Put those two ideas together and you have the inspiration for this next game. Of course, cereal maker Kellogg's is from Battle Creek, Michigan. That's why I call this one The Super Terrific Happy Battle Creek Extravaganza Game.

You know how people fill out brackets for the NCAA basketball tournament, for softball tournaments, and the like? That's what we're going to do here—with cereal.

You need two people for this game. One person has a notebook and a pen. They are The Bracket Writer. The other person is The Player.

The Bracket Writer creates a bracket with an even number of slots—similar to the brackets people fill out for the annual NCAA basketball tourney. I recommend using eight slots the first time you do it. The Player observes the cereals in the aisle, decides which ones they want in the game, and calls them out to The Bracket Writer.

The Bracket Writer puts a cereal name on each line of the bracket to create match-ups. When The Bracket Writer has the bracket filled, they update The Player that it is time for the selection process.

The Bracket Writer calls out each match-up, and The Player tells them which one is the winner. There is not a list of selection criteria. It's a subjective process that's dictated by how The Player feels about the specific cereals on this specific day. The winners move on to the next round, while the losers are eliminated. This process continues until a Grand Champion is selected.

Using 16 cereals for the game is more fun. I chose 32 cereals when I did my Super Terrific Happy Battle Creek Extravaganza, and that was crazy fun! Note that I did this later at night in the superstore.

I know, you already have questions. Yes, you can use several different flavors of the same cereal to fill out the bracket. For example, Cheerios, Honey Nut Cheerios, and Cheerios Oat Crunch could count as three different bracket entries. For fun, I visited the Cheerios website and saw 21 different types of Cheerios featured there.

Things like oatmeal, Cream of Wheat, breakfast bars, and Pop Tarts do not count as cereal. It must be cereal. It can be generic cereal, but why waste slots with generic cereal?

For added fun, The Bracket Writer can pull out the boxes of cereal in each matchup and hold them in front of The Player. The Player can pick the winner and hold up that box as the winner—sort of like when the referee holds up the arm of the winning fighter in a boxing match.

If you have a less crowded place, put the winning box on the bottom shelf to start a Winner's Row. Put the non-winning box back in its normal place. Seriously, don't just throw cereal boxes everywhere. That's poor Super Terrific Happy Battle Creek Extravaganza Game etiquette.

For added hype, you might ask a few passers-by for their opinions once you get down to the final four, or the final two, cereals. After the final match-up, crown the winner of the Super Terrific

Happy Battle Creek Extravaganza! You should also certainly think about buying a box of at least the two finalists, or maybe of all the final four cereals.

This Super Terrific Happy Battle Creek Extravaganza Game is especially fun because your tastes may change over time, even on a monthly basis. A cereal that wins one month may only make it to the final eight the next time. A cereal that was eliminated early in one game may go deep into the bracket the next time. Some cereals may fall out of the bracket and other cereals may debut in their place. The possibilities are endless.

What follows is how my Super Terrific Happy Battle Creek Extravaganza Game played out. If you don't like some of my cereals and some of these results, focus your Seinfeld Eyes and head to the store for your own game.

ROUND OF 32 MATCH-UPS

Frosted Flakes

vs.

Cocoa Puffs

Winner: Frosted Flakes

* * *

Apple Jacks

vs.

Honey Nut Cheerios

* * *

Winner: Apple Jacks

Fruit Loops
vs.
Honey Bunches of Oats

* * *

Winner: Fruit Loops

* * *

Cinnamon Toast Crunch
vs.
Reese's Puffs

Winner: Cinnamon Toast Crunch

* * *

Lucky Charms
vs.
Raisin Bran

Winner: Raisin Bran

* * *

Frosted Mini Wheats
vs.
Cap'n Crunch

Winner: Cap'n Crunch

* * *

Life

vs.
Corn Flakes

Winner: Corn Flakes

* * *

Special K
vs.
Rice Krispies

Winner: Rice Krispies

Quaker Simply Granola: Oats, Honey Raisins & Almonds
vs.
Special K Red Berries

Winner: Quaker Simply Granola: Oats, Honey Raisins & Almonds

* * *

Corn Pops
vs.
Fruity Pebbles

Winner: Corn Pops

* * *

Raisin Bran Crunch
vs.
Trix

Winner: Trix

* * *

Wheaties
vs.
All-Bran

Winner: Wheaties

* * *

Grape Nuts Flakes
vs.
Boo Berry

Winner: Boo Berry

* * *

Alpha-Bits
vs.
Corn Chex

Winner: Alpha-Bits

Golden Grahams
vs.
Golden Crisp

Winner: Golden Crisp

* * *

Cheerios

vs.

Honey Smacks

Winner: Cheerios

ROUND OF 16 MATCH-UPS

Frosted Flakes
vs.
Alpha-Bits

Winner: Frosted Flakes

* * *

Apple Jacks
vs.
Trix

Winner: Apple Jacks

* * *

Fruit Loops
vs.
Cheerios

Winner: Fruit Loops

* * *

Quaker Simply Granola: Oats, Honey Raisins & Almonds
vs.
Corn Flakes

Winner: Quaker Simply Granola: Oats, Honey Raisins & Almonds

* * *

Golden Crisp
vs.
Wheaties

Winner: Golden Crisp

* * *

Corn Pops
vs.
Rice Krispies

Winner: Corn Pops

* * *

Raisin Bran
vs.
Cap'n Crunch

Winner: Raisin Bran

* * *

Cinnamon Toast Crunch
vs.
Boo Berry

Winner: Boo Berry

ROUND OF 8 MATCH-UPS

Frosted Flakes
vs.
Boo Berry

Winner: Frosted Flakes

* * *

Apple Jacks
vs.
Golden Crisp

Winner: Apple Jacks

* * *

Fruit Loops
vs.
Raisin Bran

Winner: Fruit Loops

* * *

Quaker Simply Granola: Oats, Honey Raisins & Almonds
vs.
Corn Pops

Winner: Quaker Simply Granola: Oats, Honey Raisins & Almonds

ROUND OF 4

Frosted Flakes

vs.

Fruit Loops

Winner: Frosted Flakes

* * *

Apple Jacks

vs.

Quaker Simply Granola: Oats, Honey Raisins & Almonds

Winner: Apple Jacks

SUPER TERRIFIC HAPPY BATTLE CREEK EXTRAVAGANZA CHAMPIONSHIP MATCH-UP

Frosted Flakes

vs.

Apple Jacks

SUPER TERRIFIC HAPPY BATTLE CREEK EXTRAVAGANZA WINNER

FROSTED FLAKES

MORE INFO:
Americans eat $8.5 billion worth of cereal a year. Kiplinger.com says these are the top 19 best-selling cereal brands in the United States:

- #19: Corn Flakes

- #18: Apple Jacks
- #17: Cap'n Crunch
- #16: Raisin Bran Crunch
- #15: Reese's Puffs
- #14: Special K Red Berries
- #13: Rice Krispies
- #12: Special K
- #11: Raisin Bran
- #10: Fruity Pebbles
- #09: Life
- #08: Frosted Mini Wheats
- #07: Fruit Loops
- #06: Lucky Charms
- #05: Cinnamon Toast Crunch
- #04: Honey Bunches of Oats
- #03: Frosted Flakes
- #02: Honey Nut Cheerios
- #01: Cheerios

List of cereals spotted in Jerry's cupboard during *Seinfeld* episodes:

- Apple Jacks
- Cap'n Crunch
- Cheerios
- Cocoa Pebbles
- Cocoa Puffs
- Crispix
- Frosted Flakes
- Golden Crisp
- Golden Grahams
- Honey-Comb
- Honey Nut Cheerios
- Honey Smacks
- Lucky Charms
- Oatmeal Squares

- Oh's
- Raisin Bran
- Raisin Nut Bran
- Rice Krispies
- Trix

Sponsor

This book is made possible in part by the good folks at Specialty Models. Specialty represents some of the world's finest hand models.

Thank you.

Part V—The Search

Not wearing a *Seinfeld* shirt, but still on the lookout for some fellow *Seinfeld* fans in the grocery store? No worries, you can use the following 30 techniques to identify yourself as a *Seinfeld* fan and help strike up *Seinfeld* conversations.

30 Things To Say To Find Fellow Seinfeld Fans In The Grocery Store

- **Someone sneezes:** You say, "You're so good looking."
- **There's a bin of DVDs for sale:** You say, "I wonder if they have Rochelle, Rochelle?"
- **Toy Section:** You say, "I'm looking to get my kid an Army Pete. Have you seen one?"
- **Book Section:** You say, "Are any of these overdue from the New York Public Library?"
- **Greeting Cards:** You say, "Do they have a card for the Volcano Relief Fund For Krakatoa?"
- **Tea Section:** You ask, "Are they all out of Morning Thunder?"
- **Parking Lot:** You ask, "Are you with Dylan Murphy in the limo?"
- **Someone laughs:** You say, "Boy, that laugh sounds like Elmer Fudd sitting on a juicer!"
- **You introduce yourself to a stranger:** "Hello. I'm George Bonanza."
- **Frozen Food Section:** You ask, "Is this the pasta primavera that Mr. Dalrymple eats?"
- **Someone has a dog in the store:** You say, "Is that Snowball?"

- **Someone is walking with their child**: You say, "Is this Isosceles? You are growing like a weed!"
- **There is obvious crop dusting going on in the aisle:** You say, "I haven't smelled anything that bad since the valet stunk up my car at Kady's restaurant."
- **Salad Section:** You say, "Which one is the big salad? I need to get one for my friend Elaine."
- **You choose a person who looks scholarly:** You say, "Excuse me. Is that famous book titled *War and Peace* or *War, What Is It Good For?*"
- **Choose Your Favorite Section:** You get too close and say, "Have you seen that actor, Judge Reinhold? He's a bit of a close talker."
- **You conduct a random survey:** You say, "Who's your favorite explorer? Mine is Magellan!"
- **You stare at someone's hands:** You say, "It's you! You're the famous hand model!"
- **Bouncy Ball Section:** You say, "Can you tell me if Bette Midler ever played softball?"
- **Someone's wearing a unique top:** You say, "Is that the Gatsby Swing Top from the J Peterman catalog?"
- **Someone is obviously listening to the store's Muzak**: You say, "Is that John Germaine on the saxophone?"
- **Bakery Section:** You say, "Do you prefer chocolate babkas over cinnamon babkas?"
- **There's someone with a damaged shopping cart:** You say, "Can you tell me if JFK ever owned any golf clubs?"
- **Carpet Cleaning Machine Rental Section:** You say, "Do you know if Sunshine Carpet does a better cleaning job than these rental machines?"
- **Meat Section:** You ask, "Are you the one who traded your stereo for steaks?"
- **You see a group of teenagers:** You say, "Do you know the secret sign of the Van Buren Boys?"

- **Bread Section:** You say, "Is the strike still going on at the bagel company?"
- **In the register line:** You say, "When's the last time you saw Whitey Fisk?"
- **Hot Food Section:** You say, "Can you tell me who makes a calzone that George Steinbrenner would like?"
- **Entering or exiting the store**: You say, "The architecture of this building is exquisite. Did Art Vandelay design it?"

Part VI—The Seinfeld Catchphrases

It's my belief that *Seinfeld* launched more catchphrases into our linguistic culture than any other TV show. And it's not even close. While re-watching all 180 *Seinfeld* episodes, I kept a list of great *Seinfeld* catchphrases. It grew to more than 400 entries across a dozen or so pages in my yellow tablet. I was writing very small and sometimes sideways to fit them onto the pages. To celebrate the 30th anniversary of the show, I am listing 30 of my favorite catchphrases.

My rankings are like the stock market and change daily—sometimes hourly. You will probably start challenging this list before you get halfway through it. I know it's going to happen. It's part of what makes *Seinfeld* so great. In fact, you could choose 30 completely different catchphrases than the ones on my list and still make a compelling argument. Then you could choose 30 more completely different catchphrases and make another great argument for those as well.

30 Of My Favorite Seinfeld Catchphrases

*E*njoy this list of 30 and develop your own list. It's a lot harder to put together a list of 30 than you might think.

1. Not that there's anything wrong with that

Jason Alexander, who played the character of George Costanza on the show, says this is the most popular phrase in the series' history.

2. No Soup For You!

If you're a true Seinfeld fan, you think of this phrase almost anytime that you eat soup, think about soup, or even see soup.

3. Yada, Yada, Yada

The Paley Center called this the funniest TV phrase of all-time.

4. They're real, and they're spectacular

This is quite possibly the funniest line ever delivered by a guest star (Teri Hatcher) *on Seinfeld.*

5. Sponge-worthy

Pure Elaine magic. An instant classic! I once overheard several single ladies at my erstwhile office ranking men this way.

6. These pretzels are making me thirsty

In all of the years since that episode, I have rarely failed to think of this line when I eat pretzels—and I eat lots of pretzels.

7. Serenity Now!

When things go sideways at the office, I say these words. When traffic stinks (and it stinks a lot), I say them. When the neighbor's dog thinks it's the end of the world and won't stop barking, I say this!

8. The sea was angry that day, my friends

Jerry Seinfeld has called George's speech at the end of The Marine Biologist episode the funniest moment of the series. I think I agree!

9. No, you're Schmoopie

As you know, my wife has a love-hate relationship with this phrase because I wear it out. If that were not the case, it might have ranked even higher.

10. Are you still the master of your domain?

Spoiler alert: "The Contest" won the recent Internet poll ranking the public's favorite Seinfeld episodes. It's amazing how they could dance around the subject and then add to it by saying things like "Queen of the Castle."

11. It's a Puffy Shirt

I don't know if this phrase is funnier than "I don't want to be a pirate," but both of them are far better than Kenny Bania–branded "pure comedy gold."

12. Festivus for the rest of us

Jerry Stiller at his finest! It's even funnier when you know that Seinfeld writer Daniel O'Keefe hatched the episode idea because his father invented Festivus and they celebrated it while he was growing up.

13. Giddy Up!

Anybody can say it, but nobody says it better than Kramer. Add "Giddy up!" to anything you're about to do, and it's twice as funny!

14. Get out!

It's especially hilarious to see Elaine become increasingly more aggressive with her after-phrase pushes as the show progresses. Check out the outtakes on YouTube. I could watch a whole documentary about nothing but Elaine's Get Out activity!

15. Re-gifter

The term itself is suitably funny, but it gets extra points for making it into the culture. Re-gifting existed before Seinfeld, but there was no proper term for it. Now, even people who aren't diehard Seinfeld fans know about re-gifting.

16. Double-Dipping

It's amazing when Seinfeld could capture the essence of a problem that had gone nameless for countless decades. Finally, we were able to identify and describe this heinous activity!

17. Can't spare a square

Another Elaine gem! The whole situation is hilarious, but then I heard a hugely popular female singer tell a story where she got into this very situation.

Seinfeld World often collides with the Real World in mysterious and glorious ways.

18. Hello, Newman

If we were ranking on the basis of tone, this one might be #1. It's especially funny to hear Jerry's mom greet Newman in the same irritated way that Jerry does it.

19. Close-Talker

I had a meeting earlier in the year where the person I was meeting would stand too close to me. I had a hard time comprehending what they were saying because my brain was saying "Close Talker!" in a TV Show Jerry voice.

20. Who is this?

This one never fails and could have been used a lot more. Juxtapose frantic George talking a mile a minute over a calm, smug Jerry and it's not only a home run, it's a grand slam!

21. The jerk store called, and they're running out of you

This one is so ingrained into our culture that you don't need the whole phrase to get the meaning. I was at the airport a few years ago, and one traveler was being especially rude to another traveler. Somehow, the universe told the lady sitting next to me to shake her head, look at me, and say, "The jerk store called!" It made my day!

22. Man Hands

It's so silly that it's funny. I read where a minor league baseball team had various fan contests for a Seinfeld theme night. One of the contests centered around Man Hands.

23. Is that sort of thing frowned upon?

If "The Marine Biologist" speech is George's funniest moment, this is my nomination for his second funniest moment. My biggest disappointment with the recent social media poll was that "The Red Dot" did not make the list.

24. You gotta see the baby

Again, tone is everything. It's somewhat funny to begin with, but add the tone and Elaine's funny facial expressions, and the humor ascends new heights.

25. Helllll-ohhhhhh

I think this one is underrated, even here. I truly think the episode may have changed the entire Hello Game. That statement is true, according to the seven people I unscientifically surveyed before typing this item.

26. Low-Talker

First, you get the Low Talker. Because of the Low Talker, you get The Puffy

Shirt! It's a domino effect of hilarity! Final note on this one: Don't kids pull the Low Talker bit whenever they need to tell you something they think you don't want to hear?

27. The Pullback

Getting Frank Costanza involved in anything makes it doubly funny. You know that Jerry Stiller is actor Ben Stiller's dad, right? I immediately laugh whenever I see any picture of him with Ben from when Ben was a child.

28. And you want to be my Latex salesman?

Sometimes the visual is as funny as the actual phrase. When George comes running out of the bathroom and falls because his pants are around his ankles, it is the perfect catchphrase setup. I wonder how many takes it took before Jerry could say the line without laughing.

29. Shrinkage

Another challenge that's been around for ages that Seinfeld was able to identify and define. It's also another great dance where they were able to say what they meant without really saying it.

30. I'm Art Vandelay

Here's what can happen if you don't watch enough Seinfeld. My son works in sales. This past month, his co-worker cold-called a client and got what he thought was a very positive response. The man was ultra-friendly and referred him to the key decision maker in the organization—Art Vandelay. My son's co-worker thanked him, recorded the information, hung up, and went about googling Art Vandelay so as to be properly prepared when he contacted him. Of course, Google quickly showed him that he'd been bamboozled. I would add that this is a good hint that he needs to watch more Seinfeld episodes.

Part VII—The Seinfeld Fan Quizzes

Alright, it's time to put your *Seinfeld* knowledge to the test. You say you have a lot of *Seinfeld* Game, but can you prove it? What follows are three levels of *Seinfeld* quizzes. The fun starts with an Experts-Only Quiz. I must warn you that this quiz gets a bit ridiculous at times, because it asks for obscure numbers and other difficult things. You are a real ace if you get lots of these questions correct.

Next, it's the Medium Difficulty Quiz. You should do a lot better on this one than on the Experts-Only quiz.

If that one still seems a little tough, I threw in the Easier *Seinfeld* Quiz. Hopefully that one will make you feel like a *Seinfeld* genius.

Some of you will immediately say that you are not good at taking tests (or quizzes), and you freeze under the pressure of fill-in-the-blank questions. So, just for you I created the *Seinfeld* Multiple Choice Quiz.

Each of these quizzes has 30 questions to celebrate 30 years of *Seinfeld*. Each individual quiz is followed by its answer key.

Challenge your family and friends to see who can answer the most *Seinfeld* questions correctly. Good luck!

The 30-Question Experts-Only Seinfeld Quiz

 ood luck!

1. What mile marker is at Kramer's stretch of adopted highway?

2. How many people did Elaine mistakenly say died in the Civil War?

3. What is the number of Jerry's storage unit?

4. What are the two scores Elaine gets on the IQ tests she takes for George?

. . .

5. What apartment number does Becky Gelke, the blonde girl Jerry tries to date after his current girlfriend hits her car, live in?

6. What code do the police officers use when Jerry and George are riding in the back of their car in LA?

7. What was the last name of the male flight attendant who was mean to Elaine?

8. When Rudy Giuliani's specimen gets contaminated, what do they say is his cholesterol number?

9. What is The Maestro's real first and last name?

10. Why did the FBI shoot Jerry in Season 2?

11. How much did the older couple pay for the painting of Kramer?

12. What is the phone number for Vandelay Industries?

13. On which date did Keith Hernandez make an error and then allegedly spit on Kramer and Newman?

14. What is the number of the hospital room where Kramer sees a Pig Man?

· · ·

15. How old was the guy Elaine was dating and whom she called "vibrant"?

16. What is Jerry's license plate number?

17. When did Susan's grandpa build the cabin?

18. What is the cost of the sable hat that Elaine puts on the Peterman account?

19. While lost in the mall's parking garage, where did Kramer store the air conditioner that he had purchased?

20. How much cash did George give Elaine for her birthday?

21. What is the name of the doctor who is the ASS MAN?

22. How much money is in George's wallet when the woman handcuffs and robs him at the hotel?

23. How long does Jerry think a blind date would last if people said whatever they thought?

24. What time is it when Uncle Leo takes Jerry's parents to the airport?

. . .

25. How many pairs of underwear does George own?

26. What is the name of Kramer's friend who eats horse all the time?

27. What model number is the mannequin who looks like Elaine?

28. What is the name of the off-Broadway play that George tells NBC he wrote?

29. How much money does Kramer's old roommate owe him?

30. What is Newman's apartment number?

The 30-Question Experts-Only Seinfeld Quiz (Answers)

*H*ow did it go? Here's the answer key.

1. Mile 114

2. 620 million

3. 715

4. 85, 151

5. 4M

6. 519

. . .

7. Snyder

8. 375

9. Bob Kolb

10. For stealing cable

11. $5,000

12. KL5 8383

13. June 14, 1987

14. 1937

15. 66

16. JVN 728

17. 1947

18. $8,000

. . .

19. Purple 23

20. $91

21. Dr. Howard Cooperman

22. $8

23. 13 seconds

24. 12:22 pm

25. 40

26. Jay Reimenschneider

27. TR6

28. La Cocina

29. $240

30. 5E

The 30-Question Medium Difficulty Seinfeld Quiz

*N*o pressure, but Cousin Jeffrey answered most of these correctly.

1. What does George think he'd be worth as a gigolo?

2. What is the exact number of "I Love Lucy" episodes that Jerry has seen?

3. What is the name of Jerry and George's softball team?

4. What was the name of the restaurant where Kramer saw Joe DiMaggio?

5. What TV show does Kramer say he used to watch that always had commercials for a truck-driving school in it?

. . .

6. What is the name of the softball team that Bette Midler plays for?

7. Elaine causes trouble when she wears which other baseball team's hat when she watches a game at Yankee stadium?

8. What type of shirt does Jerry say the "authentic blacksmith" at Colonial Williamsburg wears?

9. Jerry says this position is one of the better jobs you can get with the police department.

10. What's the name of the air conditioner that Kramer helps Jerry get?

11. What was the TV show that George watched before he thought he had a heart attack?

12. Where did Kramer's friend Bob Sacamano get a job that gave him samples?

13. Why is George fired from the job Elaine got him at her office?

14. What does the Bubble Boy's dad do for a living?

. . .

15. To which celebrity does George tell the cat story when he is backstage at *The Tonight Show*?

16. Which city is called "the pesto of cities" on the show?

17. What is George's ATM code?

18. What's the name of the scotch Jerry gives Kramer?

19. What's the name of the kid whom Jerry accidentally tells that his dad is closing the family's store?

20. Where does Elaine say she met her pretend bullfighter boyfriend?

21. What is the dollar value of Susan's doll collection?

22. What's the name of the movie that Jerry shoots with the video camera?

23. What does George say his name would be if he was a porno star?

24. What gives the horse from the Handsome Cab gas?

25. What name does Crazy Joe Davola keep calling Elaine?

. . .

26. George broke a statue singing which song when he was 10 years old?

27. What is Kramer's fake name when he calls 976 numbers?

28. What was the name of the character Kramer played on Murphy Brown?

29. With whom did Kramer say he played backgammon in Grand Cayman?

30. What type of record does Jerry say George's foul-mouthed wedding toast sounded like?

The 30-Question Medium Difficulty Seinfeld Quiz (Answers)

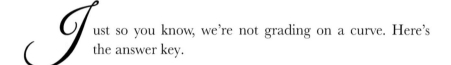

*J*ust so you know, we're not grading on a curve. Here's the answer key.

1. $300.

2. Zero

3. Friends O' Clyde

4. Dinky Donuts

5. Gomer Pyle

. . .

6. Rochelle, Rochelle The Musical

7. Baltimore Orioles

8. Def Leppard

9. Chalk Outline Guy

10. Commando 8

11. Coronary Country

12. Condom factory

13. Having sex with the cleaning lady on his desk

14. He drives a Yoo-hoo delivery truck.

15. Corbin Bernson

16. Seattle

17. Bosco

• • •

18. Hennigan's

19. Matthew

20. Switzerland

21. $2.6 million.

22. Death Blow

23. Buck Naked

24. Beef-A-Reeno

25. Netta

26. MacArthur Park

27. Andre

28. Stephen Snell

29. Elle MacPherson

. . .

30. Redd Foxx

5

The 30-Question Easier Seinfeld Quiz

*R*ight about now, you are saying, "I wish I had watched a few more *Seinfeld* episodes before I took these quizzes." No worries, this next one is easier than the first two quizzes. Notice how I call them quizzes and not tests. This whole book is about having *Seinfeld* fan fun. Quizzes can be breezy and fun to take, especially when you see them on social media. Tests, however, do not usually register very well on the fun meter. Enough talk, here's the next *quiz*.

1. What was the name of Jerry and George's high school?

2. Instead of Costanza, what name did George's gym teacher, Mr. Heyman call him?

3. What made Elaine laugh as she watched George's girlfriend's piano recital?

. . .

4. What famous person was in Elaine's aerobics class?

5. What is the name of the movie that George failed to rewind?

6. What nickname did Jerry give his favorite t-shirt?

7. What's the name of the coughing dog on the show?

8. What's the name of the dummy in Kramer's apartment?

9. What type of soup does Elaine feed her geriatric boyfriend when he's recovering from a heart attack?

10. What did George see that led to him getting caught not being the master of his domain by his mother?

11. Elaine jokes that she's going on a space shuttle mission to where?

12. What is Elaine's nickname at the office after she sends out her Christmas card?

13. Who interviewed Jerry on *The Today Show*?

14. What toy did Jerry have as a kid instead of a G.I. Joe?

· · ·

15. Newman has a mail bag from whom?

16. Which character said they would rather lick the food off the floor than eat movie hot dogs?

17. What book did George struggle to read after he joined the book club?

18. Who talked on the tape recorder Jerry was using to record his standup show at the club?

19. What famous baseball figure is on George's talking keychain?

20. Which famous actor plays Tony the Mechanic?

21. Which famous person did Kramer meet that garnered him the line "These pretzels are making me thirsty" in a movie?

22. What game does George play with the Bubble Boy?

23. What did Jerry write on the picture for his dry cleaner?

24. What song is playing when Elaine proves she can't dance?

25. What does Jerry say Gandhi loved?

· · ·

26. Kramer and Newman plan to go to this state because it has a ten-cent bottle deposit.

27. Instead of "Costanza," what last name do they use at the Chinese restaurant to try and tell George he has a phone call?

28. Kramer pitches a cologne scent idea. What does it smell like?

29. Where does Jerry get Lena's phone number?

30. What's the name of the parking place that lets hookers use its customer's cars?

The 30-Question Easier Seinfeld Quiz (Answers)

*H*ow did it go? Did you kick it into gear, or is your Jon Voight car full of *Seinfeld* knowledge no more?

1. JFK High School

2. "Can't Stand Ya"

3. Pez Dispenser

4. John F. Kennedy, Jr.

5. Rochelle Rochelle

6. Golden Boy

. . .

7. Smuckers

8. Mr. Marbles

9. Yankee Bean

10. Glamour magazine

11. Mars

12. Nip

13. Bryant Gumble

14. Army Pete

15. Son of Sam, David Berkowitz

16. Elaine

17. Breakfast at Tiffany's

18. Elaine

. . .

19. Phil Rizzuto

20. Brad Garrett

21. Woody Allen

22. Trivial Pursuit

23. I'm very impressed.

24. Shining Star by Earth, Wind & Fire.

25. Triscuits

26. Michigan

27. Cartwright

28. The beach

29. From the AIDS Walk list.

30. Jiffy Park

7

The 30-Question Seinfeld
Multiple Choice Quiz

*W*ant a tip to help you with this next multiple choice quiz? *Seinfeld* fans answer an average of four more questions correctly when they take this quiz while wearing a David Puddy-style Magic 8-Ball jacket.

1. Rochelle Rochelle is the story of a young woman's strange erotic journey from _____ to _____.

A. College to adulthood
B. Minsk to New York
C. Harlem to Milan
D. Rags to Riches
E. None of the above

2. What was the price quoted to put the squirrel to sleep?

A. $1 million
B. 80 cents
C. $1,000
D. 53 cents
E. $10

3. What year did Jerry allegedly take out the book *Tropic of Cancer* and not return it?

A. 1971
B. 1972
C. 1981
D. 1961
E. None of the above

4. What was Elaine carrying when the gang got lost in the parking garage at the mall?

A. "Sweet Buttery Brooklyn" popcorn
B. Condoms her boyfriend was scared to buy
C. A case of Today's Sponge birth control
D. A goldfish
E. All of the above

5. What TV show did Elaine write a sample script for that Jerry and George find when they are snooping around her apartment?

A. Mad About You
B. Cheers
C. Murphy Brown

D. Friends

E. Gilligan's Island

6. What's the name of the musical that wins a Tony Award and Kramer walks to the stage with the winners and accepts one for himself?

A. Rochelle Rochelle

B. Death Blow

C. Cats

D. Scarsdale Surprise

E. Phantom of the Opera

7. What song is Newman singing when his mail truck catches on fire?

A. Three Times A Lady

B. Disco Inferno

C. Take This Job And Shove It

D. Harper Valley PTA

E. Desperado

8. What is the real first name of Jerry's girlfriend whom he calls "Schmoopie?"

A. Snoopy

B. Jenna

C. Sidra

D. Marla

E. Sheila

9. What does David Letterman call Jerry?

A. Sein-field
B. Jimmy
C. A two-bit comedy hack
D. Ol' One Joke Pony
E. The reason I can't sleep at night

10. If Elaine changed her name, what would she call herself?

A. Nip
B. Elantra The Magnificent
C. Dancie McDance Dance
D. Liza
E. Dionne

11. What is the "Rolls Royce of Wheel Chairs?"

A. The Cougar 9000
B. The Jiffy Roadster
C. The Boca Raton Flash
D. Newman's New Mail Truck
E. Jerry's Grandma's Pinto

12. George tells Mr. Penske this was his college nickname.

A. The Architect
B. Mr. Automatic

C. Ol' Churn 'Em and Burn 'Em
D. The Little Engine That Could
E. The Little Bulldog

13. What's the name of the ride Jerry went on at Coney Island?

A. The Super Duper Looper
B. Superman
C. El Toro
D. The Millennium Force
E. The Cyclone

14. What's the name of the building where Jerry lives?

A. The Dakota
B. Central Park West
C. The Shelley
D. El Dorado
E. Central Park South

15. Who threw a snowball with a rock in it at Kramer?

A. Jerry
B. Elaine
C. The Pig Man
D. FDR
E. Bob Sacamano

16. What magazine does Tim Watley surprisingly have in his waiting room?

A. Glamour
B. Penthouse
C. Hustler
D. Bomb Maker's Digest
E. Russian Mail Order Brides

17. What kind of computer does Elaine have at her J Peterman office?

A. "A huge piece of crap"
B. "The latest IBM thingy"
C. A slide rule
D. Gateway 2000
E. Apple II E

18. What was the name of the bar where Elaine hung out with Keith Hernandez?

A. Fitzpatrick's Bar & Grill
B. Studio 54
C. The Player's Club
D. Champions Sports Bar
E. Scores

19. Which movie or TV show makes Jerry fail the polygraph test?

A. Superman III

B. Melrose Place
C. Superman II
D. Star Wars
E. Knot's Landing

20. What is the total amount of all the checks from the Super Terrific Happy Hour that Jerry has to constantly endorse?

A. 7 cents
B. $1.33
C. 12 cents
D. 79 cents
E. None of the above

21. What is Susan's middle name?

A. Deuteronomy
B. Biddle
C. Oligschlaeger
D. Harold
E. She has no middle name

22. Whose signature is on the giant bat outside Yankee Stadium?

A. George Steinbrenner
B. Mickey Mantle
C. Joe DiMaggio
D. Reggie "Mr. October" Jackson
E. George Babe Ruth

23. How long is Jerry's streak of not vomiting?

A. 11 months, two days, and four hours
B. 366 days—it was leap year
C. 13 years
D. 6 days—just before Festivus
E. 2 years

24. What did George have in his teeth during a job interview?

A. Pez candy from Jerry's dispenser
B. Pretzels that made him thirsty and ruined the interview
C. Bubble gum
D. Spinach
E. None of the above

25. When Kramer and Jerry see a new baby, who does Kramer say the baby looks like?

A. Lyndon Johnson
B. Abraham Lincoln
C. Jerry
D. Jerry's cousin Jeffrey
E. Jerry's dad, Morty Seinfeld

26. What is the name of the restaurant where a lot of couples break up?

A. Pomodoro
B. Sad Cafe
C. The Chinese Restaurant
D. See You Later, Alligator
E. All of this is made up—none of the above

27. What song plays on the show when Mr. Pitt fires Elaine?

A. Teen Angst (Time of Your Life) by Green Day
B. Coward of the County by Kenny Rogers
C. Blitzkrieg Bop by Ramones
D. See You Later, Alligator by Bill Haley & His Comets
E. The Way We Were by Barbra Streisand

28. What is the name of the Action News TV anchor who reports that Kramer is a suspect in the Smog Strangler Slayings?

A. Keith Morrison
B. Connie Chung
C. Peter Jennings
D. Linda Kramer
E. Elaine Seinfeld

29. What movie does Jerry's girlfriend Nina plagiarize in the episode "The Letter?"

A. Kramer vs. Kramer
B. Neil Simon's Chapter Two
C. Star Wars
D. Rocky III

E. Rochelle Rochelle

30. How many dates does Jerry say it takes to qualify for a mandatory face-to-face breakup?

A. 10
B. 5
C. 13, "The Baker's Dating Dozen"
D. 6
E. 7

The 30-Question Seinfeld
Multiple Choice Quiz (Answers)

I hope you had as much fun taking the multiple choice quiz as I had making it. Here's the answer key.

1. E: None of the above
2. B: 80 cents
3. A: 1971
4. D: A goldfish
5. C: Murphy Brown
6. D: Scarsdale Surprise
7. A: Three Times A Lady
8. E: Sheila
9. B: Jimmy
10. E: Dionne
11. A: The Cougar 9000
12. E: The Little Bulldog
13. E: The Cyclone
14. C: The Shelley
15. D: FDR
16. B: Penthouse

17. D: Gateway 2000
18. A: Fitzpatrick's Bar & Grill
19. B: Melrose Place
20. C: 12 cents
21. B: Biddle
22. E: George Babe Ruth
23. C: 13 years
24. D: Spinach
25. A: Lyndon Johnson
26. A: Pomodoro
27. E: The Way We Were by Barbra Streisand
28. A: Keith Morrison
29. B: Neil Simon's Chapter Two
30. E: 7

Sponsor

This book is made possible in part by the good folks at Sanalac Rest Stop Supply Company.

Thank you.

Part VIII—The Extra Information

Rabid *Seinfeld* fans may already possess slam dunk knowledge of these next 30 facts. See how many of these you already know. Many of these are great Happy Hour conversation starters.

The 30 Things You May Not Know About Seinfeld

1. Jerry is the only character to appear in all of the episodes of the show. Elaine was not in the pilot episode. George did not appear in the third episode of the third season, "The Pen."

2. Actor John Randolph played George's dad, Frank Costanza, the first time the character appeared on the show. Actor Jerry Stiller played Frank Costanza the other 28 times the character appeared on the show.

3. Liz Sheridan, the actress who played Jerry's mom, Helen Seinfeld, once dated James Dean in real life.

4. Actor Phil Bruns played the character of Jerry's dad, Morty Seinfeld, the first time Morty appeared on the show. Actor Barney Martin played Morty the next 23 times he appeared on the show.

. . .

5. Actor Harris Shore played the character of Mr. Lippman when the character first appeared in the episode "The Library." Actor Richard Fancy played Mr. Lippman the other 10 times the character appeared on the show.

6. Real-life Yankees owner George Steinbrenner actually shot some scenes for the last episode of the 1995 *Seinfeld* season, but they ended up getting cut from the episode. Larry David said he had to call George Steinbrenner and tell him the footage didn't work, and they weren't going to use it. He said Steinbrenner was a big boy and took it well.

7. Stand-in Norman Brenner appeared in 28 *Seinfeld* episodes. That's more than Morty and Helen Seinfeld.

8. According to Jerry Seinfeld, the near-nihilistic characters on *Seinfeld* are all rooted in his love for Abbott and Costello and their TV series "The Abbott and Costello Show."

9. Jerry dated 73 different women over the course of 9 seasons and 180 episodes.

10. Kramer made 389 entrances on the show.

11. In the early scripts, George's name was Bennett. He was originally supposed to be another comedian.

12. Jerry mentions having a sister in the episode "The Chinese Restaurant." We never see her or hear about her again.

. . .

13. The character of Kramer is based on Larry David's neighbor in New York. Kramer was originally called "Hoffman" and then "Kessler" before settling into Kramer. Jerry refers to Kramer as "Kessler" in the pilot.

14. Larry David participated in a real contest like the one in "The Contest." It lasted several months, and Larry won.

15. The real person who inspired the character of The Soup Nazi, Al Yeganeh, once insulted Jerry when he had gone out with the writers to grab some lunch. Yeganeh voiced displeasure with the show and asked Jerry to apologize in front of the whole restaurant. Jerry did an over-the-top fake apology. Yeganeh started The Original Soupman packaged foods.

16. Actors who auditioned or were considered for the part of George included Steve Buscemi, Danny DeVito, Kevin Dunn, David Alan Grier, Brad Hall, Nathan Lane, Larry Miller, Chris Rock, and Paul Shaffer.

17. Actors who auditioned for the part of Elaine included Patricia Heaton, Megan Mullally, and Rosie O'Donnell.

18. As part of the agreement to use his name, the real Kenny Kramer is allowed to bill himself as "The Real Kramer." As of 2020, Kramer is in his 24th year of hosting Kramer's Reality Tour, a three-hour bus tour that takes people to famous *Seinfeld* show-related places in New York. You can find out more at kennykramer.com.

. . .

19. In the Season 3, Episode 9, called "The Nose Job," '80s siren Tawny Kitaen played the part of an actress dating Jerry. Jerry finds her attractive, but rude and irritating. He likens the conflict between them to a chess match. Kitaen appeared in several '80s videos for the band Whitesnake, including those for hits such as "Here I Go Again, "Still of the Night," and "Is This Love." She was briefly married to Whitesnake's lead singer, David Coverdale. She also dated Ratt guitarist Robbin Crosby and pre-scandal O.J. Simpson.

20. Newman never had a first name on the show. Viewers thought they'd discovered it in the second part of the Season 7 episode "The Bottle Deposit." The farmer's daughter yells, "Goodbye, Norman" to him. We later found out the actress made a mistake and mistook "Newman" for "Norman." The producers thought the mistake was funny and kept it in the show.

21. Jerry's address is mentioned several times in the series as 129 W. 81st street, but the awning of the building says "757." What's more, the postcard shots of the building's exterior were that of a building in Los Angeles.

22. Long before her *Seinfeld* days, Julia Louis-Dreyfus was married, at age 20, to former *Saturday Night Live* comedian Brad Hall. They are still married today.

23. All of Larry David's voicework, such as George Steinbrenner, is uncredited on *Seinfeld*. He's the boxing referee, the soap opera direc- tor, the subway announcer, and the person who says, "Is anyone here a marine biologist?"

· · ·

24. Peterman's first name on *Seinfeld* is "Jacopo." The real J. Peterman's first name is "John."

25. Before *Seinfeld*, Michael Richards got a call back on his audition for the part of Al Bundy in *Married With Children*. Of course, the role eventually went to Ed O'Neill.

26. M&M's and Life Savers turned *Seinfeld* down when the show was looking for a candy to use in the episode "The Junior Mint."

27. Director Steven Spielberg said he got so depressed while filming *Schindler's List* that he watched tapes of *Seinfeld* to cheer himself up.

28. The episode "Male Unbonding" (Season 1) is the only *Seinfeld* episode title that doesn't start with the word "the."

29. NBC offered to pay Jerry Seinfeld $5 million per episode to make a 10th season of the show. Jerry turned down the offer, walking away from an estimated $110 million (22 episodes).

30. To help keep George Costanza's character as annoying as possible, Jason Alexander's wardrobe for the role was often made one size too small.

Part IX—The Actors

Now, let's take a look at the *Seinfeld* actors. We'll take a look at them in several ways:

- 30 Famous People Who Played Themselves on *Seinfeld*
- 30 (+71) More Actors Who Guest-Starred On *Seinfeld*
- 30 *Seinfeld* Guest Stars Who You May Consider to be Regular Cast Members
- 30 *Seinfeld* Actors Who Have Left Us Since the Show Ended

The 30 Famous People Who Played Themselves On Seinfeld

1. Candice Bergen
    2. Corbin Bernsen
3. Ruth Cohen
4. Jim Fowler
5. Kathie Lee Gifford
6. Rudy Giuliani
7. Bryant Gumbel
8. Keith Hernandez
9. Derek Jeter
10. Mario Joyner
11. Jay Leno
12. David Letterman
13. Roger McDowell
14. Bette Midler
15. Paul O'Neill
16. Regis Philbin
17. Geraldo Rivera
18. Al Roker
19. Fred Savage
20. Jerry Seinfeld (does it count?)

21. Buck Showalter
22. George Steinbrenner (scene cut)
23. Danny Tartabull
24. Marisa Tomei
25. Mel Torme
26. Alex Trebek (voice)
27. Jon Voight
28. Raquel Welch
29. George Wendt
30. Bernie Williams

The 30 (+71) More Actors Who Guest-Starred On Seinfeld

1. Ian Abercrombie
   2. Sandy Baron
   3. Kristin Bauer
   4. Drake Bell
   5. Tobin Bell
   6. Lloyd Bridges
   7. Wilford Brimley
   8. Michael Chiklis
   9. Melinda Clarke
   10. Jennifer Coolidge
   11. Kari Coleman
   12. Dan Cortese
   13. Courteney Cox
   14. Peter Crombie
   15. Marcia Cross
   16. Suzanne Cryer
   17. Kristin Davis
   18. Thomas Dekker
   19. Peter Dinklage
   20. Ileana Douglas

21. Lisa Edelstein
22. David James Elliott
23. Cary Elwes
24. Jon Favreau
25. Neil Richard Flynn
26. Warren Frost
27. Janeane Garofalo
28. Brad Garrett
29. Kyle Gass
30. Ana Gasteyer
31. Brian George
32. Jamie Gertz
33. Chaim Girafi
34. Lauren Graham
35. John Gries
36. Kathy Griffin
37. Anna Gunn
38. Mariska Hargitay
39. Phil Hartman
40. Teri Hatcher
41. Jon Hayman
42. Robert Hooks
43. Gordon Jump
44. Carol Kane
45. Mary Jo Keenen
46. Catherine Keener
47. Daniel Dae Kim
48. Tawny Kitaen
49. Peter Krause
50. Katherine LaNasa
51. Jane Leeves
52. Charles Levin
53. Charlotte Lewis
54. Sam Lloyd
55. Shelley Long
56. Lori Loughlin

57. Jon Lovitz
58. Paula Marshall
59. Stephen McHattie
60. Mike McShane
61. Lisa Mende
62. Debra Messing
63. Mark Metcalf
64. Christa Miller
65. Phil Morris
66. Megan Mullally
67. Brian Doyle-Murray
68. David Naughton
69. Chelsea Noble
70. Sheree North
71. Bob Odenkirk
72. Patton Oswalt
73. Chris Parnell
74. Scott Patterson
75. Amanda Peet
76. John Pinette
77. Jeremy Piven
78. Brian Posehn
79. Marty Rackham
80. James Rebhorn
81. Judge Reinhold
82. Denise Richards
83. Stephen Root
84. Debra Jo Rupp
85. Rob Schneider
86. Molly Shannon
87. Sarah Silverman
88. Rena Sofer
89. James Spader
90. Ben Stein
91. French Stewart
92. Peter Stormare

93. Brenda Strong
94. Danny Strong
95. Christine Taylor
96. Lawrence Tierney
97. Stephen Tobolowsky
98. Daniel von Bargen
99. Susan Walters
100. Shannon Whirry
101. Jim Zulevic

The 30 Seinfeld Guest Stars You May Consider To Be Regular Cast Members

1. Ruth Cohen (Ruthie Cohen, Monk's Cashier) 101 episodes

2. Wayne Knight (Newman) 48 episodes

3. Larry David (Steinbrenner's voice & more) 38 episodes

4. Estelle Harris (Estelle Costanza) 29 episodes

5. Heidi Swedberg (Susan Ross) 29 episodes

6. Jerry Stiller (Frank Costanza) 28 episodes

7. Liz Sheridan (Helen Seinfeld) 24 episodes

. . .

8. Barney Martin (Morty Seinfeld) 23 episodes

9. John O'Hurley (J Peterman) 22 episodes

10. Len Lesser (Uncle Leo) 15 episodes

11. Richard Herd (Matt Wilhelm) 12 episodes

12. Peggy Lane (Waitress) 12 episodes

13. Patrick Warburton (David Puddy) 11 episodes

14. Richard Fancy (Mr. Lippman) 10 episodes

15. Lee Bear (George Steinbrenner body) 10 episodes

16. Lauren Bowles (Waitress) 9 episodes

17. Ian Abercrombie (Mr. Pitt) 8 episodes

18. Danny Woodburn (Mickey Abbott) 7 episodes

19. Bob Balaban (Russell Dalrymple) 7 episodes

. . .

20. Steve Hytner (Kenny Bania) 7 episodes

21. David Blackwood (Beck) 7 episodes

22. Phil Morris (Jackie Chiles) 6 episodes

23. Peter Crombie (Crazy Joe Davola) 6 episodes

24. Joe Urla (Dugan) 6 episodes

25. Lawrence Mandley (Larry, Monk's Mgr.) 6 episodes

26. Sandy Baron (Jack Klompus) 6 episodes

27. Bryan Cranston (Dr. Tim Watley) 5 episodes

28. Grace Zabriskie (Mrs. Ross) 5 episodes

29. Warren Frost (Mr. Ross) 5 episodes

30. Daniel von Bargen (Mr. Kruger) 4 episodes

4

30 Of The Seinfeld Actors Who Have Left Us Since The Show Ended

*A*t first glance, it seems out of place to put together a list of actors who have died within the pages of a humor book. Since *Seinfeld* is celebrating its 30th birthday, however, I often hear people ask questions about different characters, such as "Where are they now?" and "Are these actors still alive?"

The following list is meant to celebrate these fine actors. Some are household names, while others may require you to jog your memory a bit. No matter what, one of the huge yardsticks for acting success, even 30 years later, is having guest-starred on *Seinfeld*. All of these actors are part of that prestigious club. Let's commemorate them and thank them for all the joy and laughs they brought us.

AUTHOR'S NOTE:

As this book was being finalized, I discovered a far more comprehensive list of Seinfeld actors who have passed on. It is located on IMDb. I apologize to those not listed here. Please consult the IMDb list to pay tribute to all of those Seinfeld actors.

. . .

1. Barney Martin (Morty Seinfeld) 1923-2005

2. Daniel von Bargen (Mr. Kruger) 1950-2015

3. Lloyd Bridges (Izzy Mendelbaum) 1913-1998

4. Ruth Cohen (Ruthie Cohen) 1930-2008

5. Jim Fowler (himself) 1930-2019

6. Warren Frost (Mr. Ross) 1925-2017

7. Phil Hartman (Voice in "The Package") 1948-1998

8. James Rebhorn (Mr. Hoyt) 1948-2014

9. Mel Torme (himself) 1925-1999

10. Len Lesser (Uncle Leo) 1922-2011

11. Ian Abercrombie (Mr. Pitt) 1934-2012

12. Glenn Shadix (Apartment Owner, Harold) 1952-2010

. . .

13. Sandy Baron (Jack Klompus) 1936-2001

14. George Steinbrenner (Yankees' Owner) 1930-2010

15. Gordon Jump (George's boss) 1932-2003

16. Sheree North (Kramer's Mom) 1932-2005

17. John Pinette (Carjacking victim) 1964-2014

18. Charles Levin (Mohel) 1949-2019

19. Lawrence Tierney (Elaine's Dad) 1919-2002

20. Gina Mastrogiacomo (Prostitute) 1961-2001

21. Holly Lewis (The Dinner Party guest) 1965-2012

22. Paul Gleason (Cushman) 1939-2006

23. Billye Ree Wallace (Nana) 1925-1999

24. Bill Erwin (Sid) 1914-2010

. . .

25. Edward Winter (Mr. Stevenson) 1937-2001

26. Lewis Arquette (Leapin' Larry) 1935-2001

27. Frances Bay (Mrs. Choate) 1919-2011

28. Kathryn Joosten (Betsy) 1939-2012

29. Louan Gideon (Mrs. Hamilton) 1955-2014

30. Jim Zulevic (Bernie) 1965-2006

Part X—The Episode Checklist

As a kid, writing in books was frowned upon at my school. Here, I encourage it! What follows is a checklist of *Seinfeld* episodes for you. Review it and put an "X" or check mark, or the word "Hellll-ohhhh," or whatever you want next to the ones you've watched.

Have you seen all 180 episodes? If so, you get to feel superior by checking off all the episodes and considering yourself a part of "The 180 Club." Stay tuned, and I'll give you more information about "The 180 Club" a little bit later in this book.

You can also use this checklist in many other ways.

- Put the exact number of times you've seen each episode on the line next to it.
- Settle arguments about the season number of select episodes.
- Check off your favorite episodes of each season.
- Find out which episodes you are missing in your DVD, DVR, or iTunes *Seinfeld* episode collection.
- Keep this list handy so that you can check off episodes you watch when the show makes its debut on Netflix.

- Rank episodes within a season.
- Yada, yada, yada.

Season One (1989-1990)

1. The Seinfeld Chronicles _____

2. The Stake Out _____

3. The Robbery _____

4. Male Unbonding _____

5. The Stock Tip _____

NOTES

FAVORITE EPISODE:

FAVORITE CATCHPHRASES:

Season Two (1991)

1. The Ex-Girlfriend _____

2. The Pony Remark _____

3. The Jacket _____

4. The Phone Message _____

5. The Apartment _____

6. The Statue _____

7. The Revenge _____

. . .

8. The Heart Attack _____

9. The Deal _____

10. The Baby Shower _____

11. The Chinese Restaurant _____

12. The Bus Boy _____

NOTES

FAVORITE EPISODE:

FAVORITE CATCHPHRASES:

Season Three (1991-1992)

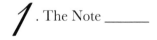. The Note _____

2. The Truth _____

3. The Pen _____

4. The Dog _____

5. The Library _____

6. The Parking Garage _____

7. The Café _____

. . .

8. The Tape _____

9. The Nose Job _____

10. The Stranded _____

11. The Alternate Side _____

12. The Red Dot _____

13. The Subway _____

14. The Pez Dispenser _____

15. The Suicide _____

16. The Parking Space _____

17. The Fix-Up _____

18. The Boyfriend _____

19. The Limo _____

. . .

20. The Good Samaritan _____

21. The Letter _____

22. The Keys _____

NOTES

FAVORITE EPISODE:

FAVORITE CATCHPHRASES:

Season Four (1992-1993)

1. The Trip, Part One _____

2. The Trip, Part Two _____

3. The Pitch _____

4. The Ticket _____

5. The Wallet _____

6. The Watch _____

7. The Bubble Boy _____

. . .

8. The Cheever Letters _____

9. The Opera _____

10. The Virgin _____

11. The Contest _____

12. The Airport _____

13. The Pick _____

14. The Movie _____

15. The Visa _____

16. The Shoes _____

17. The Outing _____

18. The Old Man _____

19. The Implant _____

. . .

20. The Junior Mint _____

21. The Smelly Car _____

22. The Handicap Spot _____

23. The Pilot _____

NOTES

FAVORITE EPISODE:

FAVORITE CATCHPHRASES:

Season Five (1993-1994)

1. The Mango _____

2. The Puffy Shirt _____

3. The Glasses _____

4. The Sniffing Accountant _____

5. The Bris _____

6. The Lip Reader _____

7. The Non-Fat Yogurt _____

. . .

8. The Barber _____

9. The Masseuse _____

10. The Cigar Store Indian _____

11. The Conversion _____

12. The Stall _____

13. The Dinner Party _____

14. The Marine Biologist _____

15. The Pie _____

16. The Stand In _____

17. The Wife _____

18. The Raincoats _____

19. The Fire _____

. . .

20. The Hamptons _____

21. The Opposite _____

<u>NOTES</u>

FAVORITE EPISODE:

FAVORITE CATCHPHRASES:

Season Six (1994-1995)

1. The Chaperone _____

2. The Big Salad _____

3. The Pledge Drive _____

4. The Chinese Woman _____

5. The Couch _____

6. The Gymnast _____

7. The Soup _____

. . .

8. The Mom and Pop Store _____

9. The Secretary _____

10. The Race _____

11. The Switch _____

12. The Label Maker _____

13. The Scofflaw _____

14. The Highlights of 100 _____

15. The Beard _____

16. The Kiss Hello _____

17. The Doorman _____

18. The Jimmy _____

19. The Doodle _____

. . .

20. The Fusilli Jerry _____

21. The Diplomat's Club _____

22. The Face Painter _____

23. The Understudy _____

NOTES

FAVORITE EPISODE:

FAVORITE CATCHPHRASES:

Season Seven (1995-1996)

1. The Engagement _____

2. The Postponement _____

3. The Maestro _____

4. The Wink _____

5. The Hot Tub _____

6. The Soup Nazi _____

7. The Secret Code _____

. . .

8. The Pool Guy _____

9. The Sponge _____

10. The Gum _____

11. The Rye _____

12. The Caddy _____

13. The Seven _____

14. The Cadillac _____

15. The Cadillac, Part Two _____

16. The Shower Head _____

17. The Doll _____

18. The Friar's Club _____

19. The Wig Master _____

. . .

20. The Calzone _____

21. The Bottle Deposit _____

22. The Wait Out _____

23. The Invitations _____

NOTES

FAVORITE EPISODE:

FAVORITE CATCHPHRASES:

Season Eight (1996-1997)

1. The Foundation _____

2. The Soul Mate _____

3. The Bizarro Jerry _____

4. The Little Kicks _____

5. The Package _____

6. The Fatigues _____

7. The Checks _____

. . .

8. The Chicken Roaster _____

9. The Abstinence _____

10. The Andrea Doria _____

11. The Little Jerry _____

12. The Money _____

13. The Comeback _____

14. The Van Buren Boys _____

15. The Susie _____

16. The Pothole _____

17. The English Patient _____

18. The Nap _____

19. The Yada Yada _____

. . .

20. The Millennium _____

21. The Muffin Tops _____

22. The Summer of George _____

NOTES

FAVORITE EPISODE:

FAVORITE CATCHPHRASES:

Season Nine (1997-1998)

1. The Butter Shave _____

2. The Voice _____

3. The Serenity Now _____

4. The Blood _____

5. The Junk Mail _____

6. The Merv Griffin Show _____

7. The Slicer _____

. . .

8. The Betrayal _____

9. The Apology _____

10. The Strike _____

11. The Dealership _____

12. The Reverse Peephole _____

13. The Cartoon _____

14. The Strong Box _____

15. The Wizard _____

16. The Burning _____

17. The Book Store _____

18. The Frogger _____

19. The Maid _____

. . .

20. The Puerto Rican Day _____

21. The Clip Show _____

22. The Finale _____

NOTES

FAVORITE EPISODE:

FAVORITE CATCHPHRASES:

Sponsor

This book is made possible in part by the good folks at The Human Fund.

Thank you.

Part XI—The 800 Club

How many of the 180 episodes did you check off? Are you part of the group that has watched all 180 episodes, maybe even multiple times for each one? You're eligible to be a part of The 180 Club!

Show off your Seinfeld prowess by downloading The Official 180 Club certificate. Get it free from my website at mentalkickball.com. You'll also receive the free weekly Fun Stories Universe humor newsletters.

Don't delay, I want to interact with you, a certifiable *Seinfeld* enthusiast, today!

Part XII—The Show Rankings

As you probably know, it's very difficult to rank your favorite episodes of *Seinfeld*. Like my list of favorite *Seinfeld* catchphrases, my list of favorite episodes can vary from day to day. That's why I found it particularly interesting when the official *Seinfeld* social media sites conducted a fan vote of the show's top 30 episodes to help celebrate the show's 30th anniversary.

"The Contest" topped that poll. This episode is always ranked near the top of almost any *Seinfeld* episode poll. It's a very funny episode that deserves this distinction. When you put together a list of 30 episodes, however, it gets very subjective. And very tough to sort out. Some episodes that I like to watch over and over did not make this list. A few examples are "The Red Dot," "The Pick," and "The Fusilli Jerry."

I invite you to start your own top 30 list. I keep mine on my Google Drive. I sometimes adjust it after I watch an episode. It's great fun for me to examine the list frequently to see if I want to make any changes. On my top 30 list, I also log 8–10 episodes below the list of 30 that I think are the closest to cracking the countdown. I sincerely hope you can create your own *Seinfeld* fun in a similar manner.

What follows is the rundown of the top 30 episodes from the official *Seinfeld* social media sites, plus a sampling of *Seinfeld* rankings from several other sources. In addition, we'll look at how my Fun Stories Universe reader newsletter folks ranked the episodes in Part XIII.

1

The Results of the 2019 Official Seinfeld Social Media Fan Vote of the Show's Top 30 Episodes

id your favorites make the cut?

(30) The Serenity Now (Season 9)
(29) The Bubble Boy (Season 4)
(28) The Limo (Season 3)
(27) The Butter Shave (Season 9)
(26) The Puffy Shirt (Season 5)
(25) The Airport (Season 4)
(24) The Race (Season 6)
(23) The Summer of George (Season 8)
(22) The Library (Season 3)
(21) The Yada Yada (Season 8)
(20) The Betrayal (Season 9)
(19) The Dinner Party (Season 5)
(18) The Outing (Season 4)
(17) The Switch (Season 6)
(16) The Fire (Season 5)
(15) The Little Kicks (Season 8)

(14) The Junior Mint (Season 4)
(13) The Rye (Season 7)
(12) The Parking Garage (Season 3)
(11) The Gum (Season 7)
(10) The Hamptons (Season 5)
(9) The Chinese Restaurant (Season 2)
(8) The Chicken Roaster (Season 8)
(7) The Strike (Season 9)
(6) The Boyfriend (Season 3)
(5) The Merv Griffin Show (Season 9)
(4) The Opposite (Season 5)
(3) The Marine Biologist (Season 5)
(2) The Soup Nazi (Season 7)
(1) The Contest (Season 4)

Breakdown of the Top 30 episodes according to seasons

- Season 1, 0 episodes
- Season 2, 1 episode
- Season 3, 4 episodes
- Season 4, 5 episodes
- Season 5, 6 episodes
- Season 6, 2 episodes
- Season 7, 3 episodes
- Season 8, 4 episodes
- Season 9, 5 episodes

Breakdown of the Top 10 episodes according to seasons

- Season 1, 0 episodes
- Season 2, 1 episode
- Season 3, 1 episode
- Season 4, 1 episode

- Season 5, 3 episodes
- Season 6, 0 episode
- Season 7, 1 episode
- Season 8, 1 episode
- Season 9, 2 episodes

Breakdown of the Top 5 episodes according to seasons

- Season 1, 0 episodes
- Season 2, 0 episodes
- Season 3, 0 episodes
- Season 4, 1 episode
- Season 5, 2 episodes
- Season 6, 0 episodes
- Season 7, 1 episodes
- Season 8, 0 episodes
- Season 9, 1 episode

2

TV Line's Ranking Of The 30 Best Episodes

*W*hat do you think of these rankings?

(30) The Abstinence (Season 8)
(29) The Barber (Season 5)
(28) The Comeback (Season 8)
(27) The Fusilli Jerry (Season 6)
(26) The Junior Mint (Season 4)
(25) The Stall (Season 5)
(24) The Library (Season 3)
(23) The Chicken Roaster (Season 8)
(22) The Cadillac (Season 7)
(21) The Puffy Shirt (Season 5)
(20) The Face Painter (Season 6)
(19) The Wallet/The Watch (Season 4)
(18) The Little Kicks (Season 8)
(17) The Fire (Season 5)
(16) The Bubble Boy (Season 4)
(15) The Parking Garage (Season 3)
(14) The Phone Message (Season 2)

(13) The Pick (Season 4)
(12) The Implant (Season 4)
(11) The Rye (Season 7)
(10) The Soup (Season 6)
(9) The Invitations (Season 7)
(8) The Strike (Season 9)
(7) The Soup Nazi (Season 7)
(6) The Pitch (Season 4)
(5) The Opposite (Season 5)
(4) The Pen (Season 3)
(3) The Boyfriend (Season 3)
(2) The Chinese Restaurant (Season 2)
(1) The Contest (Season 4)

Variety's Top 10

*W*hat belongs here and what does not belong here?

(10) The Limo (Season 3)
(9) The Bizarro Jerry (Season 8)
(8) The Fusilli Jerry (Season 6)
(7) The Marine Biologist (Season 5)
(6) The Chicken Roaster (Season 6)
(5) The Puffy Shirt (Season 5)
(4) The Chinese Restaurant (Season 2)
(3) The Opposite (Season 5)
(2) The Soup Nazi (Season 7)
(1) The Contest (Season 4)

New Arena Top 10

*I*t's a funny episode, but it's rare to see "The Andrea Doria" listed in the top 10.

(10) The Andrea Doria (Season 8)
(9) The Fire (Season 5)
(8) The Subway (Season 3)
(7) The Contest (Season 4)
(6) The Chinese Restaurant (Season 2)
(5) The Soup Nazi (Season 7)
(4) The Parking Garage (Season 3)
(3) The Wait It Out (Season 7)
(2) The Fusilli Jerry (Season 6)
(1) The Puffy Shirt (Season 5)

Ranker Top 10

*H*ere's one that has "The Opposite" ranked at the top.

(10) The Yada Yada (Season 8)
(9) The Serenity Now (Season 9)
(8) The Merv Griffin Show (Season 9)
(7) The Puffy Shirt (Season 5)
(6) The Junior Mint (Season 4)
(5) The Hamptons (Season 5)
(4) The Soup Nazi (Season 7)
(3) The Marine Biologist (Season 5)
(2) The Contest (Season 4)
(1) The Opposite (Season 5)

Den Of Geek Top 10

*K*udos to "The Soup Nazi" for taking the top spot in this one. Also of note, "The Contest" is not ranked on this one.

(10) The Merv Griffin Show (Season 9)
(9) The Pen (Season 3)
(8) The Parking Garage (Season 3)
(7) The Muffin Tops (Season 8)
(6) The Junior Mint (Season 4)
(5) The Pez Dispenser (Season 3)
(4) The Fusilli Jerry (Season 6)
(3) The Puffy Shirt (Season 5)
(2) The Chinese Restaurant (Season 2)
(1) The Soup Nazi (Season 7)

Vulture Top 10

*L*ook at "The Subway." It finished all the way up at #2 on this one.

(10) The Secret Code (Season 7)
(9) The Summer of George (Season 8)
(8) The Old Man (Season 4)
(7) The Rye (Season 7)
(6) The Pen (Season 3)
(5) The Hamptons (Season 5)
(4) The Fire (Season 5)
(3) The Opposite (Season 5)
(2) The Subway (Season 3)
(1) The Contest (Season 4)

IMDb Screen Rant Top 10

*T*ake a look at "The Outing." It finished at #4 on this one.

(10) The Abstinence (Season 8)
(9) The Chicken Roaster (Season 8)
(8) The Hamptons (Season 5)
(7) The Merv Griffin Show (Season 9)
(6) The Bizarro Jerry (Season 8)
(5) The Marine Biologist (Season 5)
(4) The Outing (Season 4)
(3) The Contest (Season 4)
(2) The Opposite (Season 5)
(1) The Soup Nazi (Season 7)

Screen Crush Top 10

*B*oth parts of "The Pilot" are ranked on this one.

(10) The Chinese Restaurant (Season 2)
(9) The Subway (Season 3)
(8) The Implant (Season 4)
(7) The Pilot II (Season 2)
(6) The Pilot (Season 2)
(5) The Switch (Season 6)
(4) The Marine Biologist (Season 5)
(3) The Hamptons (Season 5)
(2) The Opposite (Season 5)
(1) The Contest (Season 4)

Sponsor

This book is made possible in part by the good folks at Vandelay Industries.

Thank you.

Part XIII—Fun Stories

Each week, I write Fun Stories Universe newsletters to try and inject more fun into the world. At press time, we had about 10,000 people receiving those e-mails. Shout-out to the Fun Stories Universe, which currently has people from 20 different countries!

The newsletter comes out twice a week. Monday's edition is called the Monday Relief Kit. It features jokes, music and movie news, links to free books, Monday memes, and fun facts from Curly, the Fun Stories Dog. Friday's edition is the Weekend Preview. It serves up info about new movie releases, what's new on Netflix and on Amazon Prime, *Seinfeld* fan fun, more free book links, celebrity birthdays and some adorable Curly content. Given our *Seinfeld* camaraderie, I welcome you to join us. The newsletters are free. Just go to www.mentalkickball.com and sign up. You can also e-mail me at randymidnite512@yahoo.com and put "Add Me" in the subject line.

When I heard that the official *Seinfeld* social media sites were conducting a fan vote to choose the show's 30 favorite episodes, I decided to ask Fun Stories Universe to vote for its 30 favorite episodes. We received votes from 17 countries. This helps under-score the global appeal of *Seinfeld*. I greatly enjoyed reading all of the comments. Needless to say, people are very passionate about their favorite *Seinfeld* episodes.

The top episode on this poll was "The Soup Nazi." What follows is the rundown of Fun Stories Universe's top 30 episodes. Thanks for voting, and thanks for reading the newsletters!

Fun Stories Universe Newsletter
Top 30

ome of these slots were separated by less than five votes!

(30) The Switch (Season 6)
(29) The Outing (Season 4)
(28) The Stakeout (Season 1)
(27) The Betrayal (Season 9)
(26) The Hamptons (Season 5)
(25) The Chinese Restaurant (Season 2)
(24) The Race (Season 6)
(23) The Summer of George (Season 8)
(22) The Red Dot (Season 3)
(21) The Boyfriend (Season 3)
(20) The Butter Shave (Season 9)
(19) The Dinner Party (Season 5)
(18) The Bubble Boy (Season 4)
(17) The Muffin Tops (Season 8)
(16) The Fire (Season 5)
(15) The Little Kicks (Season 8)

(14) The Opposite (Season 5)
(13) The Bottle Deposit (Season 7)
(12) The Strike (Season 9)
(11) The Fusilli Jerry (Season 6)
(10) The Puffy Shirt (Season 5)
(9) The Pez Dispenser (Season 3)
(8) The Chicken Roaster (Season 8)
(7) The Library (Season 3)
(6) The Junior Mint (Season 4)
(5) The Merv Griffin Show (Season 9)
(4) The Yada Yada (Season 8)
(3) The Marine Biologist (Season 5)
(2) The Contest (Season 4)
(1) The Soup Nazi (Season 7)

Part XIV—30 Ways To Get More Seinfeld Into Your World

Want to get more mileage out of your appreciation for *Seinfeld?* There are many ways to do it. A really fun one is using Seinfeld-related names for things such as passwords and fantasy football teams. You'll undoubtedly come up with dozens of ways to *Seinfeld* your world when you really focus. Here is a list of 30 Ways To Get More Seinfeld Into Your World to get you started.

1

More Seinfeld, Please

*H*ow many items can you add to this list?

1. Fantasy Football & All Fantasy Sports Team Names
2. Trivia Team Names
3. Book Club Names
4. March Madness Bracket Names
5. Names For Your Pet
6. Names For Your Boat
7. Names For Your Rock Band
8. Passwords For Your Computer
9. Passwords For Just About Anything Else
10. License Plates (Will your state allow ASSMAN?)
11. Wi-Fi Network Names
12. Computer Network Names
13. Building Names
14. Baby Names
15. Nicknames For Your Car
16. Restaurant Names

17. Song Names
18. Racehorse Names
19. Names You Can Write On Legal Graffiti
20. Names You Can Use For Making Reservations
21. Names You Can Hold Up At The Airport
22. Pseudonyms For Just About Any Occasion
23. Greeting Card Messages Between Seinfeld Fans
24. Netflix User Names
25. Social Media Names
26. E-Mail Names
27. Business Names
28. Fundraiser Event Names
29. Names For The App You Just Invented
30. Conference Room Name

Part XV—The A-Z List Of Fun Seinfeld- Related Names

In the last chapter, I encouraged you to get more *Seinfeld*-related names into your world. I also gave you 30 suggestions for ways to do it. Now, I want to offer you an A-Z list filled with suggestions for fun *Seinfeld*-related names that you can use for passwords, fantasy football teams, social media names, what have you.

A

- A Block of Cheese The Size of a Car Battery
- A Dog With A Glove On His Head
- A Festivus For The Rest of Us
- A Flush Like A Jet Engine
- A Full-Body Dry Heave Set To Music
- A Lot of People To Mock
- A Mystery Wrapped In A Twinkie
- A Nice Box of Scram
- A "Thank You" Under False Pretenses
- Aaron the Close Talker
- Abort!
- According To The State of New York, You Are The Ass Man
- Adam's Open-Mouthed Kiss
- Address Discrimination
- Adoption Leads To Serial Killing

- Agent Katie
- Agent Stone Shot Jerry
- The AIDS Walk List
- Airing of Grievances
- Alan is a Bad Breaker-Upper
- The Alex Family Theater
- The Algonquin Round Tables
- All Hopped Up On Cinnamon Swirls
- All I Did Was Hand Someone A Bag
- All Starches Are A Scam
- Alright, Hobo Joe
- Alright, One Whiff
- Amusement Park Body
- Amy Hooked Up With Cousin Jeffrey
- And You Want To Be My Latex Salesman
- Andora's Box
- Andrea Doria's Glory
- Angela's Hit-And-Run
- The Angry Sea
- Animated Pirates and Bears
- Ann Landers Sucks
- The Anti-Dentites
- Antonio's Cat Came Back
- Any News About China Is An Instant Page-Turner
- Anybody Can Grieve In January
- The Architects
- Are You A Religious Man?
- Arguing With T-Bone
- The Army Petes
- Art Vandelay And The Latex Salesmen
- Artie Levine's Wagon
- The Ass Men
- The Atomic Wedgies
- Audrey Won't Eat Pie
- Audrey's Nose Job

2

B

- Babe Ruth Was A Fat Old Man With Little Girl Legs
- Babu Thinks That Jerry is a Very, Very Bad Man
- The Baby-Eating Dingoes
- The Backslide
- Bania The Hack
- Barry The Chimpanzee
- Beautiful Godzilla
- Beautiful Lineswoman
- Becky Gelke's Parked Car
- Believe It Or Not, I'm Not Home
- Ben Becomes A Doctor
- Benes Loves The Baltimore Orioles
- Betsy Breaks Up With George
- Bette Midler's Softball Team
- Beyond BO
- Biddle In The Middle

- Big Bad Pig Men
- The Big Flat Noodles
- Big Head Elaine
- The Big Salads
- Big Stein's Team
- Biting Kramer's Arm
- The Bizarro World Warriors
- The Board Of Directors Has Been Indicted
- Bob Cobb Is The Maestro
- Bob Sacamano's Dream Team
- Bomb Threat
- Booing Puppets
- The Bootleggers
- Booze Is Not A Religion
- The Bosco Code
- Botched Statue of Liberty Job
- Box Or Hanger
- The Braless Wonder
- Brainy Mammal Image
- The Bran Isn't Working For Me
- Break The Ball Barrier
- Breaking Up Is Like Knocking Over A Coke Machine
- Breckman
- Brett Loves Desperado
- Brody Pirates Movies
- The Bro/Manssiere
- Bryant Gumbel Smiles at Puffy Shirts
- The Bubble Boys
- Buck Naked And The Porno Stars
- The Bug Boy
- Bulls, Bears, People From Connecticut
- The Bump-Into
- Bursting With Country-Fresh Flavor
- The Busboys
- But Are You Still Master of Your Domain?
- But I'm A Man. The Rabbi Said So.

3

C

- Cadillac Buy-Back
- Call In A Bomb Threat
- Can't Go Left
- Can't Stand Ya
- The Caped Lawyer
- Car Accident And Fashion Mannequins
- Care To Make It Interesting
- Carol Loves Jokes Like That
- Cashier Ruthie Cohen
- Castro Rambles Like Steinbrenner
- Cat Killer George
- Catalog Writer's Block
- CEO Johnny Tyler
- Cereal Famine
- The Chalk Outline Guys
- Champagne Video
- Changstein

- Chef Gail Cunningham
- Chemical Bank
- The Chocolate Bobkas
- Chunnel
- The Cigar Store Indians
- Circus Manager
- Clean the Bathtub For Karen
- The Cleavage Peekers
- The Close Talkers
- Coco's Gammy Stories
- Code 519
- Cody's Coffee Shop
- Coffee Actually Means Sex
- The Coffee Table Books About Coffee Tables
- The Colonial Williamsburg Blacksmith
- Columbus Is Eurotrash
- Come Back, One Year
- The Comebacks
- Commando Eight
- Complete Rectal Examination
- Coney Island Cyclones
- Conrad's Construction Projects
- The Consolation Guy
- Corbin Bernsen Calls George A Nut
- Corky Ramirez And The 94th Street Pachinko Players
- Coronary Country
- Cosmo
- Costanza And The Froggers
- The Costanza's Twin Beds
- Costanza's Yankees
- The Counter-Clockwise Swirls
- Cousin Douglas May Be Crazy
- Cousin Holly
- Cousin Jeffrey Is For Real
- Crazy Joe Davola And The Remote Controls
- Crazy Like A Man

- Cruise Wear
- Cry, Cry Again
- The Curse Toast
- The Cursing Kids
- The Cute Nazis
- Cynthia's Fix-Up

4

D

- Dan Is A High Talker
- Daryl Nelson Is Not Black
- Dating Decathlon
- Dating Loophole
- Dating Without Games
- David And Beth Reconciled
- David Berkowitz's Mail Bag
- David Dinkins' Name Tag Fiasco
- David Mandel's Voice Cameo
- Death Blow
- Def Leppard Shirt
- The De-Gifters
- Depoofed
- Del Boca Vista Tenants' Association
- Denim Vest
- Dentist To The Stars

- Dependent On Cub Scouts
- The Derm
- The Desperadoes
- Dewey Decimal System Scam
- Dick Accidentally Drinks Vodka
- DiMaggio's Dinky Donuts
- Dinner's For Suckers
- Dionne Benes
- Disappearing Claire
- Do You Date Immature Men?
- The Domain Masters
- Donna Chang Is Not Chinese
- Donna Likes The Cotton Dockers Commercial
- Don't Condone Snubbing
- Don't Dismiss
- Don't Insult My Toothbrush
- Don't Put Your Tongue On The Floor
- Don't Skip The Swank
- The Double Dippers
- Doug The Cop
- Dr. Abbott Is A Normal-Sized Human
- Dr. Howard Cooperman's License Plate
- The Drake Is Good
- Dream Café
- Drive Slow And Sit Low
- Drop All The Pee Pipe Stuff
- Drunken Orgy of Violence
- Duncan Meyer Got Cheated
- Dwayne Got Off Sugar
- Dwayne's Sugar Relapse
- Dylan Murphy And The Limo Riders

5

E

- Earl Haffler Bets on Airplanes
- Earth, Wind & Fire's Shining Star
- Eat Hickory
- Eating A Candy Bar With A Knife And Fork
- Ed Roidlick Knows Advertising
- Eduardo Corrochio And The Matadors
- Edward R. Murrow Junior High School
- Elaine Babysits Jimmy
- Elaine Benes' Dance Party
- Elaine Opened Up Her Vault
- Elaine's IQ
- Elaine's Mall Goldfish
- Elaine's Mannequin Friends
- Ellen's Friends Kim and Melissa
- Ellen Is Perfect In Every Way
- Elmer Fudd's Laugh

- Emerald Dimples
- Emily Has Jimmy Legs
- Enzo Gives Terrible Haircuts
- Eric The Clown
- Eric The Clown Doesn't Know Bozo
- Erica, The Phone Sex Woman
- Erotic Qualities Of Salted Cured Meats
- Eva The Neo-Nazi
- Even Steven
- Evening Of Eastern European National Anthems
- Everybody Loves The Sponge
- Everything Comes Down To Toilet Paper
- Everything Goes With Naked
- Evie And The Cleaning Crew
- The Exclamation Points!
- Excuse Rolodex

6

F

- Face-To-Face Breakup
- The Fake Phone Numbers
- Families Going To War
- The Fancy Astronaut Pens
- Fans Of The English Patient
- The Fantasy Football Chronicles
- Farfel The Loud Dog
- The FBI Shot Jerry
- FDR's Snowballs With Rocks
- Feldman Brings Groceries
- The Festivus Airing Of Grievances
- The Festivus Feats Of Strength
- The Festivus Pole
- Fifth Floor With Don Ramsey
- First Class Tia
- Fitted Hat Day
- Fitzpatrick's Bar & Grill

- Fogel's A Fake
- Food And Sex—These Are My Two Passions
- Food From My Pocket
- The Fornicating Gourmet
- Forty Pairs of George's Underwear
- Fragile Frankie Merman
- Fraid Not
- Frank Costanza Speaks Korean
- Frank Costanza's Cape-Wearing Lawyer
- Frank Refused To Take Off His Shoes
- Frank's Foot Odor Problem
- Frantic Tony The Mechanic
- Fred Savage Runs Away
- Fred Yerkes Can't Remember Elaine
- Friends O' Clyde
- Friends Of The Urinater
- Friendship Level Jumping
- FROLF
- From Subbing To Kissing
- Fruit's A Gamble
- Fugitive Sex
- The Fusilli Jerrys
- Fussy Pants

7

G

- Gammy! Gammy! Gammy!
- Gammy's Getting Upset
- Gandhi's Triscuits
- The Gatsby Swing Tops
- Gavin's Dog Is A Vicious Monster
- Genderson's Murderer's Row
- Gene's The Opposite Of George
- Gennice Dropped Her Hot Dog
- George Bonanza
- George Costanza's Great Big Wallet
- George Is A Body Suit Man
- George Is Dating A Convict
- George Is Getting Frustrated
- George Is More Interested In Science Than Sex
- George Likes Naps

- George Pays Full Price For Glasses
- George Sleeps Under His Work Desk
- George Steinbrenner Loves Calzones
- George Steinbrenner's Grandkids
- George Steinbrenner's Voice
- George Wendt Gets Annoyed
- George's Gigolos
- George's Incriminating Voicemails
- George's Talking Keychain
- Geraldo Rivera Trial Reports
- Get Out On A High Note
- Get Rid Of The Exclamation Points!
- Giddy Up!
- Gillian Has Man Hands
- Gino Can Fix Your Haircut
- Girls' Bones Found
- Give Me Something I Can Use
- Give My Best To Hinckley
- Glamour Magazine's Gonna Get Ya
- Going To The Bathroom In Front Of A Lot of People
- The Golden Boys
- Gomer Pyle's Truck Driving School
- A Good Old-Fashioned Cat Fight
- Good Posse
- Goodbye, George. I Hate You.
- Government-Funded Pathetic Friend
- Government Is Parents For Adults
- Greeting Problems
- Gum Guy
- Gum Is Like A Stationary Bike For Your Jaw
- Gwen Is A Two-Face

8

H

- Hal Kitzmiller's Bad Back
- The Half-Turns
- Hammer Time
- The Hand Models
- Hang On To Her Like Grim Death
- Hanky Won't Apologize
- Happy New Year In March
- Hard Labor Fantasy Camp
- Harold & Manny The Apartment Managers
- Harry Fong's Pagliacci Ticket
- Hate The Drake
- Having Sex On Your Parents' Bed
- He Looked Like A Bit Of A Dandy
- Heavy Denim
- He'll Sew Your Ass To Your Face

- Hello, Newman!
- Hellooo…
- Hennigan's Odorless Wonders
- Here's Your Christmas Card
- Here's Your Fantasy Football Team
- He Doesn't Like To Do Everything
- He Recycled This Gift
- He Took It Out
- He Wants To Install Kramer In A Puppet Regime
- He Was Shouldering
- He's 1/64th Mayan
- He's A Bad Breaker-Upper
- He's A Dunker
- He's A Happy Camper
- He's A High-Talker
- He's A Real Bounder
- He's A Real Fancy Boy
- He's A Real Sidler
- He's Curtailed His Auto-Erotic Activities
- He's Humped His Last Leg
- He's Never Guilted
- He's Turned Me Into A Screener
- High Culture Bugs Bunny Cartoons
- High Five
- His Mother Was A Mudder
- Holding Out For Less Money
- Holy Cow
- Honolulu Luggage Handlers
- Hookers Turning Tricks In My Car
- The Hoppers
- Hot And Heavy
- How About I Put You On My Speed Dial
- How About Loni Anderson
- How Could You Spend $200 On A Tip Calculator?
- Howard Metro's Team

- Howie's Carjackers
- How's Life On The Red Planet
- The Human Fund

9

I

- I Agreed To Wear This
- I Can't Crack This One
- I Can't Have A Drop-Down
- I Can't Spare A Square
- I Choose Not To Run
- I Could Do Hard Time For This—And Community Service
- I Didn't Buy Anything
- I Do A Leave-Behind
- I Don't Care For Jewelry On Men
- I Don't Even Really Work Here
- I Don't Know What To Tell You, Elton
- I Don't Trust Men In Capes
- I Don't Want Any Sweet Action
- I Don't Want Free Coffee
- I Don't Want To Be A Cowboy
- I Don't Want To Be A Pirate

- I Don't Want To Be A 32
- I Feel Like An Out-Of-Work Porn Star
- I Finally Found A Way To Sleep In My Office
- I Got Shushed For Desperado
- I Gotta Get On That Internet
- I Grab Their Boom Box And I Chuck It Into The Ocean
- I Guess It's On My Resume
- I Guess We Could Use Some Food In Our Lovemaking
- I Had A Soft-Boiled Egg And A Quickie
- I Hate Everybody
- I Have Never Had Living-Room Naked
- I Have To Get Off Jockey Shorts
- I Have To Sit Here Like An Animal
- I Heard They Found A Family In Your Freezer
- I Love Cell Block D
- I Love Edmund Fitzgerald's Voice
- I Love Just Seeing You And Having Sex
- I Need More Pledge
- I Punched Mickey Mantle In The Mouth
- I Slept With Elaine Last Night
- I Think I See A Nipple
- I Think I Would Like To Play With Dolls
- I Think I'm At The Vortex Of The Universe
- I Think It Moved
- I Want To Go To The Tractor Pull
- I Will Not Tolerate Infestation
- I Will Show You The Stooges
- Idiots
- I'd Like To See You Get Really Mad
- If Anything Happens Here, Can I Count On You
- If You'll Excuse Me, I'm Going To Make Love To Your Mother
- I'll Just Eat Some Trash
- I'll Supply The Hat
- Impeach Morty Seinfeld

- I'm A Great Quitter
- I'm A Joke Maker
- I'm A Van Guy
- I'm All Awkward Pauses
- I'm Bomb-able
- I'm Busting
- I'm Claude Seinfeld
- I'm Darin
- I'm Frank Costanza's Lawyer
- I'm Having Sex With The Cousin
- I'm Heightening
- I'm Keith Hernandez
- I'm Like A Phoenix Rising—From Arizona
- I'm Like A Sexual Camel
- I'm No Cat Killer
- I'm Not A Waffler
- I'm Not An Orgy Guy
- I'm Not Anti-Virgin
- I'm Not Netta
- I'm Off Bread
- I'm Off Hot Water
- I'm Off The Project
- I'm Out, Baby!
- I'm Pro Foot
- I'm Still Collecting Checks—I'm Just Not Delivering Mail
- I'm Taking This Kid To The Top
- I'm The Bad Boy
- I'm The Wiz
- I'm Tucking
- Importer/Exporter
- Improv Softball
- Innocent Bystanders
- IQ 145
- Is Anyone Here A Marine Biologist?
- Is It A Titleist?

- Is This Mouth Vacuum Thing For Real?
- Isabel's Phone Number
- Isosceles
- It Cannot Not Be Funny
- It Was A Wild Scene
- It Was An Isolated Sexual Incident
- It Wasn't A Pick, Tia!
- It'll Be A Funky Adventure
- It's A Festivus Miracle
- It's A Peach
- It's A Rat Hat
- It's A Rental, But I've Had It For 15 Years
- It's Showbiz—Everybody Stinks
- It's A Write-Off
- It's Been Great Having You On The Show
- It's Gore-Tex
- It's In The Vault
- It's Not A Pet, It's A Wild Invalid
- It's Not A Puree, It's European
- It's Not A Valet, It's A Protégé
- It's Over For Bozo
- It's The New Format—Scandals and Animals
- It's The Wood That Makes It Good
- I've Been Waiting For Me To Come Along
- I've Been Waiting For This My Whole Life
- I've Got The Body Of A Taut, Pre-Teen Swedish Boy
- Izzy Mandelbaum Says It's Go Time

10

J

- J Peterman's Exquisite Team
- Jack Is The Wiz
- Jack Kennedy's Broken Golf Clubs
- Jack Klompus Hates Morty Seinfeld
- Jacopo Power
- Jake Jarmel's Glasses
- The James Bond of Laundry
- Jane Cannot Spare A Square
- Jane Wells Live At The Scene
- Janet Looks Like Jerry
- Java World
- Jay Riemenschneider Eats Horse
- Jay Scott Greenspan
- Jayne Mansfield Had Some Big Breasts

- The Jerk Store
- The Jerk Store Called
- The Jerk Store Is Running Out Of You
- Jerome
- Jerry Cheats When He Runs
- Jerry Cougar Mellencamp
- Jerry Dumped Movie Marcia Brady
- Jerry Goes To Camp With Frankie
- Jerry, Hello
- Jerry Seinfeld Is The Devil
- Jerry Wants To Date A Chinese Woman
- Jerry's Bike Just Hangs There
- Jerry's Cereal Killers
- Jerry's Dating Assistant
- Jerry's Pet Parakeet
- Jerry's Sister
- JFK High School Alumni Association
- JFK's Golf Clubs
- JFK's Temper
- Jiffy Dump Wants No Stumps
- Jiffy Park Hookups
- Jimmy Holds Grudges
- Jimmy Likes This Team
- Jimmy Seinfeld
- Jimmy's Gonna Get You, Kramer!
- Jodi Won't Massage Jerry
- Joe Hollywood
- Joel Rifkin May Be A Serial Killer
- John Germaine And The Jazz Players
- John Grossbard And The Old Roommates
- The Johnson Rods
- The Jon Voight Car Is No More
- Jon Voight's Car
- The Journey From Milan To Minsk
- Joy Boy
- Judaism For The Jokes

- Judge Arthur Vandelay
- Julianna The Massage Therapist
- June 14, 1987
- The Junior Mints
- JVN 72

K

- The K Men
- Karen Really Wanted Kramer
- Karl The Exterminator
- Karma—No, it's Kramer
- Katya The Romanian Gymnast
- The Kavorka
- Kel Varnsen Is Not Real
- Kenny Rogers' Roasters
- Kessler
- Kevin The Bizarro Jerry
- Key Brothers
- Key Privileges
- The Key Word Is Tasteful
- The Keys Movie Script
- Kim's Korean Nail Parlor
- KL5 8383
- Krakatoa Volcano Relief Fund

- Kramer Completely Funked Up My Mattress
- Kramer Fights Children
- Kramer Likes the Bottom
- Kramer Loves Canadian Football
- Kramer Vomited On Her
- Kramerica Industries
- Kramer's Adopted Highway
- Kramer's Karate Kids
- Kramer's Mafia Girlfriend Connie
- Kramer's Mary Hart Seizures
- Kramer's Slicer
- Kramer's Tony Award
- Kramer's Traded Stereo
- Kramer's Whole Life Is A Fantasy Camp
- Kruger Doesn't Care
- Kruger Industrial Smoothing

L

- Label Me Thankful
- Lady Kerry
- Lanette's Dude
- The Large Clown Shoe Firefighters
- Larry David Is Not Amused
- Larry David Is Wicked Rich
- Larry David Will Quit The Show
- Larry David's Voice
- The Last War Fought In Wigs
- Latvian Orthodox
- Laura The Lip Reader
- Laura's Engaged
- Le Trianon
- Learn My Name, Letterman
- Legally I Could Marry Your Daughter

- Let Me Ask You A Question
- Let's All Wear Nametags
- Let's Go For The Green
- Let's Push This Giant Ball Of Oil Out This Window
- Let's Start The Insanity
- Lewd, Lascivious, Salacious, Outrageous!
- Library Cop
- The Library Fines
- Like A Martian
- Like Rubberman
- Like Taking Candy From A Baby
- Like Talking To Aunt Sylvia
- Like You're Dating USA Today
- Lin Nicademo's Gout
- The Lip Readers
- Little Jerry Seinfeld
- The Little Kicks
- Little Miss Candy Bar
- Living In A Jar With A Couple of Holes Punched In The Top
- Living In The Galapagos Islands With The Turtles
- The Lizard Guy
- Lloyd Braun and the Crazy Crew
- Lois
- Lomez Is Going To Miss The Movie
- Look Away, I'm Hideous
- Look Out, Everybody! I'm Working With Pills.
- Look To The Cookie
- The Loppers
- Lords Of The Manor
- A Lot of Stars From The 70s Were Not Hygienic
- The Low Talkers
- Lt. Joe Bookman Is Not Amused
- The Lumbar Yard

13

M

M

- Mabel Choate Loves Marble Rye
- The Mackinaw Peaches
- The Mad Architects
- The Made-Up Boyfriends
- Magellan And The Favorite Explorers
- The Magic Loogies
- Magic Pan Crepe Restaurants
- The Male Body Is Like A Jeep
- Makeup Sex
- Making Out During Schindler's List
- Man Hands
- The Man Makes A Pretty Strong Bird
- Man, That's Some Tart Cider
- The Mandelbaum Three
- Mandlebaum's Gym
- The Marble Ryes

- Marcelino's Bodega
- The Marine Biologists
- Marisa Tomei Face Punchers
- Marla The Virgin
- Martin's Girlfriend Gina Likes Jerry
- Massage Teaser
- The Matadors
- Maximum Shrinkage
- Mean Mr. Benes
- Mean Mr. Hoyt
- The Melrose Place Polygraphs
- Merry Christmas—Whatever
- Michigan Loves Bottle Depositers
- Middle Manager Sid Farkus
- Mile 114
- The Mimbos
- Mom and Pop Are Childless
- The Monkey Level of Pet Ownership
- Monk's Café Mashers
- The Mononucleosis Misdiagnosis
- The Moops
- Morning Thunder
- Morty Seinfeld For President
- Moses Was A Picker
- Mother Chuckers
- Mother Nature's A Mad Scientist
- The Mother Of All Mail Days
- Movie Phone
- Mr. Kramer Projects A Rugged Masculinity
- Mr. Marbles
- Mr. Morgan Is Not Sugar Ray Leonard
- Mr. Pitt's Mustache
- Mr. Ross Loves John Cheever
- Mr. Steinfeld
- Mr. Thomassoulo
- Mr. Wilhelm's Big Project

- The Muffin Tops
- Murphy and O'Brien
- Musicians—Get A Real Job
- My Boys Can Swim
- My Boys Need A House
- My Dream Is To Become Hopeless
- My Guys Don't Know Your Guys
- My Intern From NYU
- My Little Cable Boy
- My Little Man's An Idiot
- My Mechanic Pulled A Mary Beth Whitehead
- My Name Is Dolores
- My Name Is Susie
- My Own Personal Hand Puppet
- My Phone Finger
- My Rods And Cones Are All Screwed Up
- My Son Is A Bootlegger
- My Stupidity Pays Off

14

N

- The Naked Station
- New York City Serial Killers
- Newman Gets A Sample of Jerry's Hair
- Newman Goes Postal
- Newman's Mail Truck
- The Next Millennium Must Be Jerry-Free
- No Calls The Day After That
- No Child Of Mine Is Ever Going To Be Named Seven
- No Nostril Penetration
- No Refund Joe
- No Serenity Now
- No Soup For You
- No Tell Rochelle, Rochelle
- No, You're Schmoopie
- Nobody Beats The Wiz
- The Non-Fat Doormats

- The Non-Laughers
- Noreen Loves High Talkers
- Not A Fan of the Yelling
- Not One Of Your Swing Joints
- Not That There's Anything Wrong With That
- Nothing But A Claw
- Nurse Paloma

O

- Obsessed With Cleavage
- Obsessed With Lactating Women
- Obsessed With Shoes
- Officer Vogel Is Not Amused
- Oh Henry Heiress
- Oh Moses, Smell The Roses
- Ollie Ollie Oxen Free
- One Angry Clown
- One Big Nude-A-Rama
- The One I Thought Was Julie Turned Out To Be Karen
- One Lap Around
- One Thing Led To Another
- The Ottoman Empire
- Our Meat Problems Are Solved
- The Outrageous, Egregious, Preposterous Team
- Ovaltine

P

- Pachyderm Juggles Pizza
- Pamela's Birthday Party
- The Panties Your Mother Laid Out For You
- Pants Always Beats No Pants
- The Parking Lot Prostitutes
- Party Time Is Over
- Pasta Primavera Makes Me Sneeze
- Patty Lawrence Had Orgasms
- The Pavarotti Liars
- The Penalty Strokes
- Pendant Publishing
- Pennypacker's Pricing Gun
- The Pensky File
- Pensky's Little Bulldogs
- Pete's Luncheonette
- Peterman Reality Tour

- Phase Two of the Pines of Mar Gables
- Phone Sex Workers
- Pick A Face And Go With It
- Pillage And Plunder
- The Pinky Toes
- Pity Is Very Underrated
- Pizza With Pachyderm
- Play Now
- Plaza Cable
- The Pom-Pom-Wavin' Backseat Bimbos
- The Pomodoro Breakups
- The Pony Express
- The Pool Guys
- The Pool Shrinkers
- Poor Lilly
- Poor Little Pinkus
- Poppie Didn't Wash His Hands
- Poppie Peed On This Team
- Postmaster General Henry Atkins
- The Pre-emptive Breakups
- Pretty Wild Girlfriend
- The Prickly Petes
- Problems With Woody Woodpecker
- The Produce Section Is A Very Provocative Area
- Public Fornicators
- Puddy's Face Paint
- The Puerto Rican Seinfeld Haters
- The Puffy Shirts
- Punching George In The Brain
- Purple 2

Q

- Qualities Prized By The Superficial Man
- Queen of Confrontation
- Queen of the Castle
- The Queen Is Dead
- Queens College

R

- Rachel Goldstein's Shrinkage Lesson
- Rageaholics Anonymous
- Raquel Welch Can't Dance
- Ray McKigney's Exquisite Hands
- Real And Spectacular
- Really Big TV
- Really Tiny Instruments
- Rebecca DeMornay Has A Temper
- The Red Dots
- Redd Foxx And The Wedding Toasters
- Regards Don't Mean Anything
- The Re-Gifters
- Relationship Intern
- Remembering Marvin Kessler
- Remy Loves Hepburn
- Retail Is For Suckers

- Revenge Is Very Good
- Rhode Island Beauty Queens
- The Ribbon Bullies
- Rick Levitan Does Not Recycle
- Ring Dings And Pepsi
- RIP, Chelsea
- The Robot Butchers
- Roger McDowell Did It
- Rusty's Beef-A-Reeno
- Rusty's Rickshaw

19

S

- Sagman, Bennett, Robbins, Oppenheim & Taft
- Sal Bas Is Not Salmon Rushdie
- The Salad Eaters
- Salsa
- Sandra's Panties
- Scarsdale Surprise
- Schmoopie's Revenge
- Schnitzer's Bakery
- The Screeners
- See If We Qualify As Organ Donors
- See You In The Cafeteria
- The Seinfeld Chronicles
- Seinfeld, You Magnificent Bastard
- Serenity Now
- Serenity Now, Insanity Later
- Sex In A Tub? That Doesn't Work.

- Sex On George's Desk
- Sex To Save The Friendship
- Sexual Perjury
- Sexual Rule Book
- Sharon Besser's Greatest Moment
- She Confused Six With Sex
- She Doesn't Have Toe Thumbs
- She Finds My Stupidity Charming
- She Jerry
- She Likes The Pop-In
- She Talks To Her Food
- She Was Refunding
- She's A Nazi!
- She's A Package Full of Something
- She's A Two-Face
- She's Off The Speed Dial Completely
- She's Too Good
- The Shushers
- Shut Up And Pack
- Sic Semper Tyrannis
- Sid Parks Cars
- Sidney Fields Thinks Jerry's An Idiot
- Simons' Stock Advice
- Sitting In A Tepid Pool Of My Own Filth
- Skiing Naked With A Good Hat
- Skinny Mirrors
- Slapping Hands Is The Lowest Form of Male Primate Ritual
- Sleeping With A Giant
- The Sloppy Poppies
- Smart Like A Computer
- Smells Like The Beach
- The Smelly Cars
- The Smog Stranglers
- Smuckers The Coughing Dog
- Smugness Is Not A Good Quality

- The Sniffing Accountants
- Snowball Spooks Elaine
- The Snub Is Good
- So F**cking Good
- So Much Hand I'm Coming Out of My Gloves
- Some Sort Of Medieval Sexual Payola
- Something Of Yours Has Been in The Toilet
- Something That Comes About Once In A Lifetime
- Son of Dad
- The Soup Nazis
- Specter's Fetish
- Spending The Night Is Optional
- Spite Never Sleeps
- Spinach In Your Teeth
- Sponge-worthy
- Sports Is So Pedestrian
- The Squirrel Prognosis
- Stall Man
- Standing By The Elevator Like A Dope
- Standing In For Punky Brewster
- Step Off, George
- Step-Skipper
- Stephen Snell Is In The House
- Steven Koren is Young Costanza
- Stop Crying And Fight Your Father
- Storage Unit 715
- Strangers Treating Your House Like It's A Hotel
- Street Bums Starring Mr. Heyman
- Street Toughs
- The Strike Is Over
- Stuff Your Sorries In A Sock, Mister
- Stump Trouble
- Sue Ellen Mischke's Bra
- Summer of George
- Sunshine Carpet
- Superman And Cereal

- Superman's Super Humor
- The Super Terrific Happy Hour
- The Susan B. Anthony Problem
- Susan's Doll Collection
- Suzie, Call Dr. Bison
- Sven Jolly
- Sweet Fancy Moses
- Swimming In Thank Yous
- Swimming In The East River
- Swimming Through A Flabby-Armed Spanking Machine
- Switzerland Bullfighters

20

T

- Take A Drink And Let Us Smell You
- Take This And Add That
- Talk Dirty To My Tape Recorder
- TCB—Takin' Care of Business
- Team Festivus For The Rest of Us
- Team Murphy Brown
- Team Pez
- Tennis Is Ping Pong Standing On The Table
- Thanks For Mutton
- That Cashier's Riding Horses On My Money
- That Kim Novak Had Some Really Large Breasts
- That Might Be Just A Tad Harsh For Women's Wear
- That Seems About Right
- That Son of a Bitch Jean-Paul
- That Story Stunk Worse Than These Chairs
- That's A Nice Four Seconds
- That's Gold, Jerry

- That's It—It's Go Time
- That's My Ass In Your Window
- That's Really The Most Important Part of the Reservation
- That's What Puts The Magic In Magic Pan
- That's Where It Gets Tricky
- The Choose
- The Go-Getters
- The Group That Goes Around Mutilating Squirrels
- There Are No Ball Men
- There's A Hair In My Farina
- There's A New Neil In Town
- There's Good Naked And Bad Naked
- There's Some Tension There
- There's Something About the Klip-Klop
- These Are Dog Pills
- These Are Sweatshop Eggs
- These Doves Were Murdered
- These Pretzels Are Making Me Thirsty
- They Like To Sell Their Own Coffee
- The Team About Nothing
- This Cantaloupe Stinks
- This Has International Incident Written All Over It
- This Is Not A Metallica Concert
- This Is Not An Easter Egg Hunt For Your Childish Amusement
- This Is One Ripping Good Yarn
- This Is The Hamlet Of Diseases
- This Is Unprecedented
- This Is Why You're Not In The Pilot
- This Team's Gold, Jerry!
- This, That and the Other
- This World Is Your Sanctuary
- Thomassoulo Thinks Turkeys Can Fly
- Those Aren't Buoys
- Those Hip Musicians With Their Complicated Shoes

- Three Times A Lady
- Throw A Dart Out The Window
- Tim Watley's Book Club
- Tim Watley's Penthouse Party
- The Timeless Art of Seduction
- Tina Likes The Couch
- Tiny Squirrel Instruments From El Paso
- Tiny Tunes
- The Tomato Hand Fruits
- The Tonsil People
- The Toxic Wedding Invitations
- Toby's Pinky Toe
- Tom Pepper Is Cosmo Kramer
- Topless Jane
- Toys
- The Tractor Story
- Trading Sleep For Sex
- Tryptophan And The Classic Toys
- Tropic of Cancer
- Tuesday Choir Practice
- Turn Your Key
- Turning The Screws On George
- Twinkies Aren't Cooked
- Two Magicians Trying To Entertain Each Other
- Tyler Chicken

U

- The Ugly Babies
- Uncle Leo's Eyebrows
- The Unshushables
- Up On 94th Street With Corky Ramirez
- The Uptight Maestros
- The Urban Sombreros
- Urinary Freedom

V

- The Van Buren Boys
- Vandelay Industries
- Vegetable Lasagna
- The Velvet Fog
- The Very Large Goiters
- The Virgins
- Vomit Streak 13
- Voodoo Jackie Chiles

W

- Wait A Second…
- Waitress/Actress
- Waking Up In The Hudson River In A Sack
- Walking Behind The Elephant With A Big Shovel
- War, What Is It Good For?
- Was That Wrong?
- Watching Joe Temple's TV
- We Don't Care, And It Shows
- We Give Up, You Think of Something
- We Need A Medical Dictionary
- We Never Saw Gail Benes
- We Never Saw George's Brother
- We Never Saw Jerry's Sister
- We Pretty Much Know What We're Doing in There
- Welcome to the Merv Griffin Show
- We'll Always Have Pancakes
- Well, I've Got Gonorrhea

- We're Back Together
- We're Broken Up
- We're Broken Up For The Rest of the Day
- We're Going To Have To Move The Whole Damn Forbidden City
- We're Not Putting Up With Head-First Parking
- We're Out Of Time
- We've Lost The Fat Man·And We're Running Lean
- We've Never Worked Together On A Lie
- What Do You Tip A Wood Guy?
- What Is This Salty Discharge?
- What The Hell Is E-mail
- What's Your Read, Stan?
- The Wheels Are In Motion
- When Do You Start To Worry About Ear Hair?
- When You're Dead, You're Dead
- Where Is Gail Benes?
- Where Were You During The Poncho Craze of '84
- Where's The Depravity
- Whiff Away
- Whitey Fisk Is For Real
- Witchy Woman
- Who Ate The Raisins?
- The Whole Concept of Lunch Is Based On Tuna
- The Whole Monetary System Is Obsolete
- Who Doesn't Serve Cake After A Meal?
- Who Leaves A Country Packed With Ponies?
- Who Told You To Put The Balm On?
- Who's Wanda Pepper
- Why Can't I Be A Soulmate
- Why Can't You Be More Like Lloyd Braun
- Why Don't You Just Tell Me The Name Of The Movie
- Why The Hell Did I Bring The Wagon
- Why Would Anybody Want A Friend?
- Willie The Dry Cleaner
- Wink If Your Team Is Good

- The Woman In The Blue Sweatpants
- Women Behind The Wheel Of Semis
- Woody Allen's Movie Neighborhood
- Worlds Are Colliding
- The Wrath of the Raincoats
- The Wyck Winks

X

- X-Rated Kid Talkers

Y

- Ya Gotta Like Magic
- Yada, Yada
- Yada, Yada, Yada
- Yada, Yada, Yada—I'm Really Tired Today
- The Yankee Beans
- Yev Kassem Is The Soup Nazi
- The Yogurt Is Non-Fat
- Yo-Yo Ma
- Yoo-Hoo Drivers
- You Are The Doofus
- You Bite It, You Bought It
- You Can't Change Your Chart
- You Can't Save Movies
- You Can't Stop Science
- You Could Serve Dinner On My Head

- You Done With Your Little Amusement
- You Don't Think I Could Put Asses In Seats?
- You Fake Erased
- You Get Me One Coffee Drinker On That Jury
- You Gotta See The Baby
- You Had These Wooden Teeth
- You Look Scrumptious
- You Play A Hell of a Piano
- You Scream Good
- You Stink
- You Think You're Better Than Me?
- You Wouldn't Last A Day In The Army
- Young Gets Promoted
- Your Car's On Fire—Merry Christmas
- Your Face Is My Case
- Your Palette's Unrefined
- You're Freaking Me Out
- You're Just As Pretty As Any of Them, You Just Need A Nosejob
- You're Killing Independent George
- You're On The Fringe of the Humor Business
- You're Out of the Loop
- You're So Good Looking
- You're The Bear Claw In The Garbage Bag of My Life
- You've Got A Tell
- You've Got Three Pints of Kramer In You, Buddy
- You've Got Yourself A Girlfriend

Z

- Zapruder's Mets' Game Spitting Film

# #

, 2, 3...

- 2 Years That Kramer's Mom Has Been Clean
- 5 Years Since Kramer Saw His Mom
- 555-8643
- 5B, Cosmo Kramer
- 5E Is Newman's Apartment Number
- 6'3", 190 Pounds—That's Cosmo Kramer
- 8-Finger Sign
- 9 O' Clock Was Kramer's Bedtime When He Was Growing Up
- 9-Year-Old Joey Zanfino
- 12 Cent Checks From Super Terrific Happy Hour
- The 12-Year Strike
- 13-Episode Commitment From Kimbrough
- 13-Year Streak Of Not Vomiting
- 17 Is George's Softball Number

- 12:22 PM, Uncle Leo Takes Jerry's Parents To The Airport
- 25 Years Inside Nana's Apartment
- 26 MLB Teams
- 32 Cent Stamp With James Dean
- 33 Cents For Lettuce
- 40 Pairs of George's Underwear
- 66 Is Vibrant
- 80 Cents To Put The Squirrel To Sleep
- 85 & 151
- 95% Of The Population Is Undatable
- 101 Episodes With Ruthie Cohen
- 103-Degree Temperature
- 165 MPH
- 200 Jewish Singles Need You
- 220 Is Kramer's Bowling Score
- 375 Is Rudy Giuliani's Contaminated Cholesterol Number
- 715 Is The Number of Jerry's Storage Unit
- 976 Andre
- 1937 Is The Room Where Kramer Sees The Pig Man
- 1947 Is The Year Susan's Grandpa Built The Cabin
- 23,000 Miles Before The Car Got Stunk Up
- 620,000,000 Died In The Civil War
- The $8,000 Sable Hats
- #1 Dad
- #2 Pitcher, Jerry Seinfeld
- #17 Catcher, George Costanza
- #17 On The Mets, Keith Hernandez
- $2 Is The Rewind Charge
- $5 Chambermaid Tip
- $8 Robbery
- $91
- $98 To Replace Rochelle
- $182

- $240 Is Owed To Kramer
- $1,900 In George's Account
- $5,000 For The Kramer Painting
- $8,000 Sable Hat
- $20,000 For Peterman's JFK Golf Clubs

Part XVI—The Future

It is now time to brainstorm more ways to get more *Seinfeld* in our lives and keep the show in our memories for many more generations. I need your help. I've listed 30 *Seinfeld* Things I'd Like To See Happen. Please peruse the items and add at least one item you'd like to see happen that would keep *Seinfeld* at the top of our minds.

The 30 Seinfeld Things I'd Like To See Happen

1. Larry David and Jerry Seinfeld should win the Lifetime Achievement Award at the Emmy Awards.

2. Lots of minor league baseball teams have had a Seinfeld Night. Major League Baseball needs to have a Seinfeld Night for all 30 teams during each season. We need to carry the idea over to the NFL, NHL, NBA, and all of the soccer leagues.

3. Netflix needs to do a "Seinfeld Behind The Scenes" show where various actors watch each of the episodes and comment about it. It would be great if Larry, Jerry, Julia, Jason and Michael could do some of them, but it would also be fun to hear from many other folks who either appeared on or worked on the show.

4. We need a yearly Seinfeld-Con where people meet, actors make public appearances and talk at panels, and where *Seinfeld* is celebrated.

. . .

5. There needs to be a Seinfeld Cruise each year with various actors from the show.

6. TBS needs to have a Seinfeld Week each year, similar to Discovery channel's Shark Week. All 180 episodes are played over the course of the week, and guest hosts from the show offer comments.

7. There needs to be a special Seinfeld Week on *Jeopardy!*

8. There needs to be a National Seinfeld Trivia Challenge with Matt and Vinnie from the Seincast podcast challenging *Seinfeld* experts. If you haven't listened to Matt and Vinnie, be sure to check them out!

9. Facebook and/or Instagram (or YouTube) should hold monthly live *Seinfeld* watch parties where someone whose been on the show serves as the host. People talk about the show and hear behind-the-scenes tidbits. Furthermore, every *Seinfeld* fan should join at least 3 *Seinfeld* groups on Facebook. Shout-out to No Seinfeld Group For You! Shout-out to Seinfeldisms! Shout-out to Seinfeld memes! Shout-out to Seinfeld's Best Bits!

10. McDonald's or another fast food place should have a Seinfeld Game where you win prizes and celebrate the anniversary of the show.

11. Seinfeld scratch-off ticket games should be licensed by all state and national lotteries.

. . .

12. A major music artist should put out an album with a Seinfeld-related name and go on a Seinfeld name–related world tour.

13. Movie theaters need to show episodes of *Seinfeld* before movie showings. A sponsor name could be placed in the top corner of the show.

14. There should be new Seinfeld-related merchandise and clothing released each year with some of the profits going to a charity. Top designers could be asked to collaborate. The same goes for bobble heads! Check out all of the *Seinfeld* baseball game giveaway bobble-head activity on eBay.

15. There needs to be a huge Seinfeld Wing at the Smithsonian. If not, we need a Seinfeld Museum.

16. There needs to be a traveling *Seinfeld* memorabilia show that stops at hundreds of cities.

17. There needs to be an entire *Seinfeld* section at a major amuse-ment park such as Disneyland or Universal Studios.

18. At preset intervals, *Seinfeld* show regulars and guests should do a takeover of the official *Seinfeld* social media sites to answer questions and give out inside information.

19. I don't want a reunion show, but there should be a *Saturday Night*

Live episode where *Seinfeld* cast members could all be guests for the week.

20. Five words: More *Seinfeld* character Halloween costumes.

21. There need to be *Seinfeld* grocery bags you can use each time you hit the store.

22. A new *Seinfeld* game for PlayStation, Xbox and/or other platforms wouldn't go amiss either.

23. New *Seinfeld* action figures aimed at desk placements in offices could actually make you *want* to go to work.

24. Funny *Seinfeld* adult coloring books—maybe one for each episode—could help us destress more effectively.

25. Three words: *Seinfeld* comic books.

26. We need a *Seinfeld* cereal, already!

27. *Seinfeld* clips could be broadcasted on gas station TV networks. Put the sponsor name in the top corner, and enjoy some laughs while you pump your gas.

28. NASA gives one of its future spacecrafts a *Seinfeld*-related name.

• • •

29. Google goes with a Seinfeld-theme each year on the anniversary of the show.

30. Every reader of this book should go to WikiSein, read lots of entries, and then add an entry of their own. After, that, head to Wikipedia and do the same thing.

Part XVII–The Bonus Stories

As a fellow *Seinfeld* fan, I wanted to give you a bonus something for reading this book. What follows are two short stories from my *Fun Stories Greatest Hits* book. In fact, they are about the grocery store. You can find this book and all of my books on Amazon.

1

How NASA Thins The Herd (The One With Kenny Rogers and the Grocery Store)

* * *

I was at the grocery store the other day and this woman in front of me in the checkout line had walked right out of the 1980s. And it wasn't the fun, *Stranger Things* version of the 1980s. She wore a "Kenny Rogers American Tour 1980" t-shirt and red parachute pants, and her hair was a very poor attempt to impersonate Farrah Fawcett.

Speaking of *Stranger Things*, she strangely seemed to enjoy frozen dinners. Her basket was inexplicably full of them. I fixated on all the different varieties of frozen dinners that slithered down the grocery store conveyor belt. I also wondered why there were no frozen pizzas in her cart.

For fun, I tried to match several of the frozen dinners with their appropriate Kenny Rogers song. I softly hummed "The Gambler," "Coward of the County," and "You Decorated My Life." I hadn't had so much interest in Kenny Rogers since the day I had found out he once dated my all-time favorite model from *The Price Is Right*, Dian Parkinson.

And then it happened.

The 80s lady dug through her huge purse, frowned, and asked for a pen so she could pay for her frozen things with a check. For me, watching people slowly write out checks at the grocery store is the equivalent of being tied up in a chair and being subjected to incessant fingernail scraping on a chalkboard. If I'm ever captured by a hostile foreign force, they wouldn't need weapons to subdue me. They just need to start slowly writing checks and follow that up by slowly updating their check register.

Even worse, she discovered, after endlessly pulling items out of her purse, that she had left her checkbook at home. I tried to maintain a safe distance from all the used Kleenex tissues she was depositing everywhere. A long line formed behind me as she ransacked her purse. Her voice quivered more and more as she declared with each item that it was not the checkbook. It was obviously not her day.

Just as I was reaching my happy place in my mind, she made eye contact with me and let out an uncomfortable sigh. This was the part where I was expected to offer her some kind of comfort phrase. I like to tell stories, but I had nothing for her that day. She had caught me at a selfish time. The pre-game for the World Series was coming on TV in less than 15 minutes; I had planned my entire day around the game.

I promise I'm better than this on most days. I did make a sad face for her and offer half a head bow, however. It probably scored very low on the comfort scale. Bottom line, I'm probably not the best candidate to write any of those "Chicken Soup for the Soul" stories.

My neighbors in line? They were far less accommodating than me. It began to rain snippy comments. The grocery store cashier began to feel the heat. Irritated, he asked the lady, "How can we resolve this?"

Checkbook Lady let out a long sniffle—I think it was mostly acting—and paused for dramatic effect. She then said, "My life is just so complicated right now that I need some of those smart people at Nassau to help me figure it out. Nassau would know what to do."

Oh my…

I briefly made eye contact with the checkout guy, but we both looked away quickly. Now, I had another dilemma. I had no idea if it was Nassau, Florida or Nassau in the Bahamas. I'm 99% certain, however, that Checkbook Lady needed a refresher course about America's space program.

To add an extra layer to this story, I had just toured NASA's Houston operation a few months earlier because my wife has relatives who work there. This was a lot to process while I was already worrying about the World Series and simultaneously beating myself up inside because I could not remember more Kenny Rogers songs. It really bugged me that the number of frozen dinners she was buying was greater than the number of Kenny Rogers songs I could remember. Casey Kasem would not be pleased.

Good news. Checkbook Lady found some cash in her purse and bought most of her groceries. She had to leave two frozen dinners behind. She headed for the exit, as those frozen dinners joined the array of items running through my mind.

Flashbacks ensued. My mom used to give me those Swanson Chicken frozen dinners when I was a kid. Random events trigger more random memories for me—most of the time.

More good news, I made it home for most of the pre-game show. Even so, I had to grab my phone and Google Up, because I'm the Freakin' Michael Phelps of Googling. Before the first pitch of the World Series baseball game, I watched the Port Nassau Webcam, read some part of the Bahamas Vacation Guide, and swiped through a slideshow of the Top 10 Must-See Attractions in Nassau.

Poor NASA.

With an opportunity to learn more about space and rocket science, I took Checkbook Lady's lead and directed the whole surfing session toward vacation destinations. Don't worry about NASA. In fact, the plot twist of this story applies to both Checkbook Lady and me. NASA is a top-level operation. It has no time for this type of nonsense. News flash! This is how NASA thins the herd.

It's not too late for you, though. How can you succeed where

Checkbook Lady and I failed? Learn more about NASA and don't ever write another check.

Now, I'm off to Google more about frozen dinners—and Kenny Rogers. I must never be flat-footed again if ever I need to remember a greater number of songs by a music artist I heard as a kid than the number of frozen food items the person in front of me is purchasing. That's my own top-level stuff. It's my private version of NASA, baby!

Speaking of "The Gambler," do you remember the episode of "Seinfeld" that had a story arc about the Kenny Rogers chicken restaurant? The bright neon light from the restaurant's sign was taking over Kramer's apartment. Yes, I had to Google it. It is from Season 8, Episode 8 and it's called "The Chicken Roaster." Alright, that's enough Kenny Rogers already.

2

Grocery Store Math

* * *

often like swinging by the grocery store after work and grabbing exactly 15 items. It's 15 items because that is supposed to be the limit on the number of items you can have in the express checkout lane. It's also a perfect amount of items to place in one of those red, handheld, carry-along baskets. This keeps you from needing the big metal grocery cart with the wheels that often roll in several different directions or lock up at inopportune moments. I love driving the big cart and filling it (sometimes with basketball shots) on a big store run, but not on a 15-item run.

While I'm stopping short of calling it grocery store terrorism, I want to report something you probably already know. New math has gained a foothold in our grocery stores. It's math we never learned in any classroom. It is not the metric system. It is not a Sting song.

What I'm trying to say is it seems that 15 items can now mean as many as 24 items. That's how many items the guy in front of me had the other day—24. And, he seemed pretty proud of it. He was the happiest guy in the store. He had no worries about being over the 15-item limit.

This is just the latest chapter in what is now a never-ending book of over-the-item limit stories that are unfolding while I stand in line. Earlier that same week in the same grocery store line, a tough guy in a half-buttoned sleeveless shirt had 22 items. He looked around with a glare just daring anybody to call him out on it.

And it's not just a guy thing. Last month, this very pleasant older lady announced to me that she was sorry that she had 17 items but her grandkids were coming over. This meant she needed some extra things, but the big cart was too heavy for her to push. What could I do but look at her, smile, and say, "It's all good." I could stomach her 17 items, but the whole process is out of whack.

I know there are real problems out there. People are homeless. Countries are fighting wars. Nobody seems to agree on politics. But interwoven into this dynamic is the fact that most all of us have to go to the grocery store.

I used to feel bad if I even thought about sneaking in a 16th item during the checkout process. Now, I think I'm one of the few people who really has 15 items. Is everybody else laughing at me because I'm playing by the rules? I feel like I have a neon "chump" sign flashing over my head that everybody in the grocery store can see except me. Does that lady even have grandkids? Do they chuckle all the way to their cars thinking about what a sucker I am for not having more than 15 items?

Where does all this madness stop? I'm betting that before I can even get this story published, somebody will break the current record of 24 items. As of now, I've never seen a store clerk call anybody out for being over the limit. Does this ever happen?

Never fear, Fun Stories Nation. I've recently gone to my happy place to deal with this grocery store madness. I have convinced myself that I am doing research for a hidden-camera show. The show awards points to shoppers for every item they successfully check out past the 15-item limit. How many items can they get before a store clerk calls them out for being over the limit?

Good game shows need a twist. Sometimes, in my pretend

grocery game show, there is a "Good Citizen Award." This happens when a person is rewarded for having exactly 15 items and not going over. I'm thinking a fun prize would be to give them 15 seconds of free shopping. That would bring positive attention to those who play by the rules.

I don't have a name for the show yet. If you have a clever name idea, please send it to us on the Facebook page or tweet it to us @mentalkickball. You can also torture me with pictures of how many items you've successfully gotten away with checking out in the 15-item line.

If you're keeping score at home, this grocery item limit is morphing into its own currency exchange rate. Right now, 15 = 24 is the way I would try to define that exchange rate.

Happy shopping!

Part XVIII—The Thank You And Adieu

I want to sincerely thank you for reading this book. As I have said before, *Seinfeld* is not just a sitcom, it's a state of mind. So keep your Seinfeld Eyes open as you travel through your days. I'd love to hear from you when you see funny things through your Seinfeld Eyes. Drop me a line anytime at randymidnite512@yahoo.com.

Don't let the insanity stop. Want more fun *Seinfeld*-inspired fan stuff? Click my mentalkickball.com website to get fun bonus material. Get an official certificate for "The 180 Club." You can also get the 30-item *Seinfeld* Fan Grocery List and the free Fun Stories Universe weekly humor newsletter. All of these bonus items are free and add extra layers to your *Seinfeld* fan fun. Don't miss them.

I'm off to watch "The Marine Biologist." Again, thank you!

SPOILER ALERT:

There may be some bonus material if you keep turning the pages. Besides, you don't want to miss the always-exciting "About The Author" section located at the end of the book.

Sample Chapter From Fun Stories Greatest Hits

Ridiculous Movie Theater Experiences: Bigfoot Popcorn

* * *

We'll start this next story by first agreeing that refreshments cost way too much at the movie theater but that it doesn't stop the majority of us from standing in slow-moving lines to hand over our hard-earned cash in exchange for popcorn, soda, candy, and many other things. This is the process I was painstakingly moving through the other day with my family. I had reached the point where I had my popcorn and was waiting at the condiment station for the man in front of me to finish using the machine that butters your popcorn. I generally love having control over the butter machine. Butter Machine Guy (BMG), however, was taking it to the extreme.

BMG kept bouncing the popcorn container up and down and then shoving it back under the butter machine spout to distribute the butter more evenly.

To properly paint the picture for you, he had purchased the ginormous upcoming blockbuster-movie keepsake bucket that doubles as a trash can and costs most people half of their month's salary. Speaking of painting, BMG was no Popcorn Picasso, but the container still looked pretty impressive in his hands.

I must say that I've been down this "let's distribute the butter evenly on our popcorn" road many times with the smaller popcorn tub. So, as a fellow butter-on-popcorn connoisseur, I tried to tell BMG that my oldest son had actually solved this problem about a year ago. You may already know this trick too. You acquire the large red straw that is usually intended for the Icee drinks. That red straw fits almost perfectly inside the spigot on the butter machine. This allows for the perfect distribution of butter, even to the deepest recesses of the popcorn bucket. This eliminates any need to toss up the popcorn as though you're making a pizza.

But as I started the story, BMG looked back at me, furrowed his brow, and gave me the stink eye like I was interrupting the most important event of his life so far. He was in no mood to chat with me, especially about his movie theater snack. Next, BMG made a grunting noise, reached out, and pulled the metal tin full of jalapenos completely out of its slot.

What the heck? I didn't know what to think. Is this a power move? Was I supposed to be impressed? BMG then began smashing the jalapenos down in the container with his left hand as he turned the metal tin sideways, which allowed him to pour out the jalapeno juice. He smashed them down harder and moved the tin around in circles so he could completely cover the butter-laden popcorn with the jalapeno juice.

Some people like to use the term "Bigfoot" when they see something they've never seen before. I've also heard the term used when people accidentally spot a celebrity. No matter which version of Bigfoot you prefer, this whole thing had officially become a Bigfoot experience for me. I kept staring at BMG's less-than-clean hands as they smashed the jalapenos to get the maximum amount of juice out of the tin.

I incorrectly surmised—and I surmise a lot, especially when I see Bigfoot in the movie theater—that he would then just put the jalapeno tin back into its slot without getting out any jalapenos. Instead, BMG completely put his other (right) hand into the metal tin and turned it into a highly useful scoop. He dutifully scooped out two heaping handfuls of jalapenos that he then dumped on top of the popcorn. It's good he bought the ginormous keepsake bucket. I couldn't quit staring; it was like watching a tennis match as my eyes bounced back and forth between the tongs that were meant for the removal of jalapenos and his large right hand scoop.

After another grunt, BMG set the jalapeno tin way over to the left—nowhere near the hole it normally lives in—and then quickly wiped both his hands on his jeans. Why? Because that's the way Bigfoot rolls. BMG stepped back a little and gave his makeshift jalapeno masterpiece a full-on stare down. He shook his head disapprovingly and deemed it not quite right. So, BMG placed his bucket on the counter and mashed the popcorn one final time—with both hands. It looked like he was about to go on a very long trip and trying to smash things into his suitcase before closing it. He then dutifully wiped his hands on his jeans for a second time, and he was gone.

The tennis match continued. Only now, I was staring back and forth between BMG walking away and the messy condiment station he had created with his Bigfoot brand of mayhem. There was butter and jalapeno juice everywhere. I was scared to look, but I knew that some of it was on the floor and that I was standing in it.

When BMG was about 10 feet away, he could sense my eyes following him. He flipped around and caught me staring at him like a pitcher picking a runner off first base. He actually growled like a horror movie villain and gave me another stink eye. Pardon the pun, but this was great theater.

I could go on for 10 more pages about all my Bigfoot-related thoughts. At that point, however, I decided to just walk across the lobby and use the other butter dispenser at the other condiment station. I had zero desire to use anything at my original condiment station. I also had to stop by the bathroom and wash my hands—for no particular reason.

What about you? Do you like jalapenos and/or jalapeno juice on your popcorn? Am I just freakin' crazy? Is BMG ahead of his time?

Final note, I was back at the same theater the other day, using the same condiment station where BMG had made his juicy jalapeno masterpiece. And guess what? The contents of the metal tin had changed. There were still jalapenos in the tin, but they were now packed in little plastic containers with lids. There was not a pair of tongs in sight.

Now, I wonder if other people are pulling the same gross jalapeno pouring trick as the stink-eyed man I had encountered. I also wonder what the people who buy nachos—the people who are really the ones using the jalapenos—think about the new plastic containers.

I also wonder—in the style of Mulder and Scully—if maybe this jalapeno situation is far bigger than I imagined. What if the nacho folks had also been "juicing" their movie snack before the big jalapeno change? And what about the pizza people? Is this why cheese is the best-selling slice? So that they can have their own jalapeno fun?

How likely is all of this? Is this a sinister plot to unnerve all of us as we seek a little solace from the real world and try to enjoy some over-priced movie snacks? I will continue to monitor the situation.

The truth is out there.

Sample Chapter From
Fun Stories For Your
Drive To Work

Happy Friday (Mr. Pee Man)

* * *

*R*obert Frost has this beautiful poem called "Stopping By Woods on a Snowy Evening." It has all of these wonderful images. This is not a similar story. It is, however, a true story.

I mention the poem because its closing line talks about having miles to go before I sleep. That's my mantra on many days as I head to work. But this story happened on a Friday, and my timing on this particular day was capital "G" glorious. It was 7:56 AM and I didn't even have to speed-walk into the building.

Painting the picture, there is this little alley that runs past the back door through which I go into my office. Your mind is picturing a dark, scary alley, but it's all very public and fairly bright. It's not scary. As I'm walking, I make eye contact with this guy on the other side of the alley. He looks surprised.

Upon further review, I see the dude is PEEING on the wall across the alley from the entrance to our back door—and it's been going on for a little while. Because I caught him by surprise, MR. PEE MAN decides to slowly start to walk away, but he's still peeing.

I can hear a soft splashing noise as it starts winding down. The stream is getting smaller and smaller.

I'm a little surprised, but also a little impressed that despite being interrupted, he's still finishing what he started. I'm thinking maybe our company needs more dedicated performers such as Mr. Pee Man. Sure, there was some of that pee stench in the air, but it was Friday. I had my iced tea in my hand. This was not going to slow me down. So, I just randomly blurted out, "Happy Friday" to Mr. Pee Man.

He's finished by now, and he, Mr. Pee Man, does a double-take and stares at me for about five full seconds. He's pondering a lot of things. Finally, he decides I'm OK and that I'm being sincere in my "Happy Friday" bit.

So, Mr. Pee Man gives me a half-salute and says in a confident, surprisingly deep, voice, "Happy Friday, man." It was my own Robert Frost type of moment! In fact, it was the best thing that happened to me that whole day.

I went inside and spent the rest of the day giving people that little half-salute and a "Happy Friday, man" in a deeper voice. Other people started doing it. Soon, most of the people on my floor were trying to imitate the deep voice, "Happy Friday, man". We don't get out much. It might even become a regular Friday thing in my office.

All of this office camaraderie happened because somebody was peeing in the alley at an unexpected time. Maybe this is how some of the best ideas get started. Do they do this at NASA? I know their astronauts can drink their own pee. Maybe I should google "crazy ways people have invented things."

I'd love to see Mr. Pee Man get an invite to the next White House summit. The results could be fascinating. Mr. Pee Man might just shake out some fresh foreign policy strategies. Talk about your Mental Kickball!

Final note, I know you're going to be peeing several times today. You probably have to go right now. For starters, don't think of me as you are doing it—that might be a little weird. Try to use that time to come up with your own office thing that might break up the day.

Think outside the box, but don't pee that way. If your boss likes your new idea, tell your boss you have a special laboratory where you go to manufacture these new ideas.

If you're listening to this on a Friday, Happy Friday, man!

iTunes/Apple Music Version

Sample Chapter From
Fun Stories For Your
Drive Home

Alright, Alright, Alright!

* * *

END OF WORK WHISTLE

Congratulations, you did it! Your workday is over! It's now time to flip the script and have some fun. A good way to shift into Fun Mode is to say the catchphrase actor Matthew McConaughey made famous when he played the character David Wooderson in the coming-of-age comedy *Dazed and Confused*. It goes, "Alright, alright, alright!"

The phrase washes away all the bad parts from your workday and helps you find your chill. It's even more fun if you imitate McConaughey's character from the movie when you say, "Alright, alright, alright!" Sometimes, on Fridays, I say it a dozen or more times as I drive out of my work parking lot.

Fun fact: The scene where McConaughey says, "Alright, alright, alright!" was the first scene he ever shot in his acting career. In fact, he wasn't even supposed to be in the scene. It took place outside a famous Austin, Texas fast-food restaurant called Top Notch *(check it out the next time you are in the ATX)*.

As he set the scene, director Richard Linklater felt like McConaughey's character would be the kind of person that would hang out at Top Notch. Linklater told McConaughey he'd like him to make an appearance in the scene even though it wasn't in the script.

McConaughey agreed to give it a try. He took a 30-minute walk to get a feel of how his character related to the scene. McConaughey asked himself, "What is David Wooderson all about?" He then decided that his character was about at least three things: his car, his rock 'n' roll music, and his pursuit of girls.

When he later entered the scene, McConaughey realized he could check off all three boxes. He was in his car; he was listening to rock music, and he was about to talk to a red-haired girl. In character, McConaughey confidently blurted out, "Alright, alright, alright!"

The phrase stuck with him. At the 86th Academy Awards, when he won the best actor award for *Dallas Buyers Club*, McConaughey stepped up to the microphone and said, "Alright, alright, alright!"

It's a phrase that helps you get into Fun Mode and prepares you for adventure. Speaking of fun adventures, I'd like to thank you for joining me for another *Fun Stories* book adventure. You can read this book in any place, at any time; but to add to the fun, I am presupposing that you are enjoying this book at the end of your workday.

Think of me as part storyteller, part game-show host, part DJ, and part madcap tour guide. I'm about to share some crazy stories about work, school, home, dating, and much more. No topic is off-limits as I seek to help you check off the boxes you need checked-off in order to have fun. You'll also be surprised by how often I can get myself into awkward and embarrassing situations.

Before the book is over, I'm going to quit the Cub Scouts, wear a police helmet backward, create an ugly scene at a soccer game for four-year-olds, witness the ultimate waitress revenge, watch my new employee mentor misbehave, and hand out a Clown Commuter Award.

It all begins right here, right now. Say it with me as you turn the page, "Alright, alright, alright!"

Sample Chapter From Searching For More Cowbell

1

Searching For More Cowbell

* * *

*E*ven as I write this, in some typical research facility with
fancy glass walls, people in goggles and white lab coats are
hard at work, trying to invent new medicines and other important
things to make the world a better place. This is not that type of situation. Our goals here at *Fun Stories* are far less lofty. All we want is
more smiles and laughs.

One of the most popular *Saturday Night Live* sketches of all-time
is "More Cowbell." Aired on April 8, 2000, it spoofed the VH1
documentary series *Behind the Music*. The sketch supposedly took us
behind the scenes of the recording session for the 1970s classic song
"Don't Fear the Reaper" by Blue Oyster Cult. SNL host Christo-
pher Walken played the part of music producer "The" Bruce Dick-
inson, and Will Ferrell played fictional BOC member Gene Frenkle.
Jimmy Fallon played the band's drummer.

As the sketch unfolded, Ferrell aggressively played a cowbell,
standing too close to the other band members as the group tried to
record the song. His exuberant style irked the other musicians.
Walken's character, however, seemed to enjoy it. He implored Ferrell

to use "more cowbell." One of Walken's great bits of dialogue in the skit went like this: "Guess what? I've got a fever, and the only prescription is more cowbell!"

The phrase "more cowbell" became a staple in my life after watching that skit. The phrase can mean many different things to the people who enjoy it. For me, the phrase pushes one to have more fun, seek more adventure, and follow their dreams at a faster pace.

Because writing for *Fun Stories* is always so enjoyable for me, I often read through my rough drafts and tell myself that I need more cowbell. This encourages me to get closer to the finish line during the writing process. I hope that this edition of *Fun Stories* will help you better define your meaning of the words "more cowbell."

There's one other inspirational detail about the "More Cowbell" skit. Even though it almost always ranks at or near the top of any list of SNL's greatest sketches, Will Ferrell had to submit the script for the skit at least seven times before it finally made it on the show. Even then, the sketch was slotted near the end of the episode, where the more offbeat sketches are often aired. The lesson here is: Believe in yourself and dance to the beat of your own drum. The world will eventually dance along.

Here at *Fun Stories*, we celebrate random, odd, and offbeat stories. I sincerely thank you for taking the time to join our party. If you want to leave a comment, you can do so on the Fun Stories Facebook page, Twitter site, or on the website, mentalkickball.com. Again, thank you. You are greatly appreciated!

Sample Chapter From
Random City Limits

Gatorade For The Soul

***

I recently read that those "Chicken Soup For The Soul" people are so successful that they might be going public and offering stock. This story has nothing to do with that, but I like to call it "Gatorade For The Soul."

This is a story about my youngest son's middle school basketball team. The story involves a bunch of really good kids who met the textbook definition of student-athletes.

You know what's coming next. You're right. They just didn't win very many basketball games.

To try and help them win games and play better defense, their young coach spent a great deal of time trying to get them to hold their ground on defense and take more charges. If you don't know already, a charge is when you play tight defense, get a foul on the other team, and make them turn the ball back over to your team.

The coach set the team goal of earning a specified number of charges before the end of the season. If they hit that number, he said he would buy all of the players a Gatorade each. Aren't middle school incentives great? He got complete buy-in and unbridled enthusiasm for his idea by offering free Gatorade!

Well, this is not "Rudy." It's not the story of the underdog rising above. In fact, the team didn't win any more games the rest of the season, but they definitely showed a lot of improvement. It all began when they started taking more charges on defense. The strategy snowballed to the point where they needed just three more charges in the final game of the season to hit their Gatorade goal.

Unfortunately, they were matched up against the top team in the league. The opponent was unbeaten and playing the game at home. The early game was brutal. How brutal? It was 16–0 in favor of the opponents. Our coach called timeout and gave a red-faced speech about how important it was to play better defense and take charges.

By halftime, however, our team was down by more than 25 points. On the bright side, however, we had taken two charges. We only needed one more for free Gatorade.

The second half saw the score get more and more lopsided. Our defense lagged, and the other team seemingly couldn't miss any shot they took. Soon, the game was in the final minute, and there wasn't a charge in sight.

Then, destiny stepped in. Remember that great moment when Team USA upset the Russians in hockey? Well, this was a thousand levels less than that, but it was still noteworthy. The opposing team, trying to tack on more baskets to inflate an already large lead, pushed the ball down the floor—right into a charge call.

When the referee made the call, my son's team—at that point down more than 40 points—jumped in the air like they just won the NBA Championship! They hugged each other, slapped hands, screamed, and actually forgot there was a game going on for about 30 seconds.

The other team was puzzled. The refs were puzzled. The opposing team's fans were puzzled. We just smiled. They had no idea that an important goal had been achieved. Moments later, the ref had to threaten to call a technical foul if our team didn't stop celebrating.

Our team began chanting "Gatorade, Gatorade, Gatorade!"

Finally, our player, who had been fouled, moved to the free throw line and promptly missed both shots. It didn't matter. Our team was still high-fiving, fist bumping, and talking about Gatorade.

Confused, the other coach called timeout. He looked around, concerned. I think he somehow thought this was the start of some evil plot that our team was about to hatch.

He had his team dribble out the rest of the time on the clock. When it was over, our guys jumped up and down again. The other team had finished an undefeated season and won the championship, but our guys were twice as happy and twice as loud. They were going to get free Gatorade!

Sample Chapter From
Fun Stories Box Set

Nobody Does Quality Control
Like A Military Parachute
Factory

*H*ow well have you been performing at work? Be honest. Are you on top of your game? Can you prove how well you are performing? Better yet, can you put yourself on the line to underscore your good performance? Compare your recent performance to this next story.

Over the years, I've learned a lot of useful things from my dad by listening to his stories about the various things that happened to him during his military career. The Army, and all of the branches of service, have a specific manner of doing things. They come up with checks and balances that sometimes cause your eyes to widen with amazement when you hear about them. This is one of those times.

On a visit home, I was grabbing a few things at the store with my dad. We saw a sign advertising a sale on a particular brand of chips. In the bin, however, was mouthwash. Was a rogue employee watching us on a hidden camera? Were we being punked? My dad made the comment, "This wouldn't happen at the parachute factory on the post (Army)."

I thought this was a random comment, even for my dad. I asked him what the parachute factory had to do with snacks or oral hygiene, and he replied, "They've solved quality control. They get the most out of their people and ensure the highest quality in their product."

This sounded like it came right out of one of the military recruitment videos. My dad is a no-nonsense guy, and I was sure they had good people and made a quality product at the military parachute factory, but I had to ask him why he was so sure about it.

"You have to jump them if you work there," he said. He went on to explain that that's what happens if you work at a military parachute factory. One minute, you're sitting there having a routine day, making parachutes; the next minute, one of your higher-ups walks by and says, "Hey, buddy. You've been randomly selected for quality control. Grab that parachute, strap it on, and you're going to jump with it."

That blew my mind. Talk about always being on your toes at work. That system will make you pay more attention. If I worked in that system, I'd surely be very diligent about each and every item.

The underwear companies think they're clever by dropping in that "Inspected by Number 17" sticker in the packages. The thought being that you feel better about the purchase and about the company because ol' Number 17 has your back on quality control.

The military parachute factory is 1,000 levels more advanced than that anonymous "Number 17," or whatever number they choose when that day approaches. Quick underwear rant, I once only got five pairs of underwear in a package that was supposed to have six. Inside, there was a sticker that said it was inspected by Number 7. I think Number 7 was eating moon pies and surfing the Internet the day he/she was supposed to be checking to make sure there were 1, 2, 3, 4, 5, 6 pairs of underwear in the package that I ultimately bought.

I did not return the package of underwear. It would have been too embarrassing to take my newly-purchased underwear to the counter and watch some random person count them one by one, see that there were just five, and then read the already-ripped-open package to make sure it said six. It would also be embarrassing if they asked me if, somehow, I was wearing the sixth one and had forgotten about it.

I don't want any part of that confrontation. I just silently felt cheated each time I put on a pair of that brand of underwear.

If your job is making parachutes at a military parachute factory, put that on your resume in bold and underline it. That experience is a magic ticket. If the next company that you interview with understands how military parachute factories work, that experience will put you at the head of the interview class.

Within reason, I'd hire someone with little or no experience in what I was looking for if I found out the applicant had experience working at a military parachute factory. I know that person is going to arrive early, work diligently, carefully plan everything, and make sure we have all of our bases covered. Plus, if we have a TV commercial or a special promotion where we need somebody to jump out of a plane with a quality parachute, they are going to hit a home run!

Tomorrow at work, pretend you are working at a parachute factory. Use that zeal to handle all of your projects.

Ducks on the Pond

Overview

Scott's 2011 book *Ducks on the Pond* is a love letter to baseball, but it's not just diamonds, dust & Dodgers. It's about youth, wonder & nostalgia. Steal away to Kool Aid-stained summer days, wiffle ball, barbecue hot dogs and "American Top 40" with Casey Kasem.

Murph uses his "storyteller mashup" style to blend "Cultural Literacy" with "Schoolhouse Rock" and take snapshots of the grand game. He morphs generations of Bronx Bombers in "Revelry In The House of Ruth," the ultimate conversation starter for Yankee Nation. Liven up your longball lingo with "The Home Run Alphabet." Take a poetic excursion to every MLB stadium & every World Series played since 1965.

The fun doesn't stop there. Count down Murphy's favorite baseball nicknames with music references as assigned by ESPN's Chris Berman. See Albert Pujols become "E Pluribus Pujols," and watch as "The Monsters Are Raging On Huston Street."

This book is a must-read for anyone that loves baseball.

Fun Stories Weekly
Humor Newsletter

1

Join the Fun!

---

* * *

*B*e a part of the Fun Stories Universe. Get the free Fun Stories Universe Weekly Humor Newsletter. Visit www. mentalkickball.com or send an e-mail with the subject "Add Me" to randymidnite512@yahoo.com.

Sponsor

This book is made possible in part by the good folks at Play Now Sports.

Thank you.

Also by R. Scott Murphy

Fun Stories Greatest Hits

Fun Stories Box Set (5 books)

Searching For More Cowbell

Fun Stories For Your Drive Home

Fun Stories For Your Drive To Work

Random City Limits

Ducks on the Pond

Fun Stories Universe Weekly Humor Newsletter

About The Author

R. Scott Murphy looks at the world in fun, sometimes twisted, ways. He's watched so many *Seinfeld* episodes that he now believes he sees some things through Seinfeld Eyes. He's the madcap mind behind the bestselling *Fun Stories* series of humorous paperbacks, eBooks and audiobooks. Part storyteller, part game-show host, part DJ, and part comedic tour guide, the award-winning author resides in Austin, Texas, with his wife, two sons, and a rescue dog named Curly, with whom he writes the weekly Fun Stories Universe humor newsletter.

Murphy holds a master's degree from the University of Missouri School of Journalism and has taught advertising at the University of Texas. At one time or another, he's been a radio personality, TV sports anchor, stadium announcer, advertising writer, marketing executive, and game show producer.

Murphy is a four-time winner of the "Late Show with David Letterman" Top 10 List Contest, plus a Remi Award winner for script writing in the film industry. He's topped the Amazon chart for humor books on six occasions and sent three of his audio singles to the top of the iTunes Comedy Songs rankings.

Besides writing books, Murphy enjoys spending time with his family, watching *Seinfeld* episodes, announcing baseball games, attending sports events, and collecting copies of the classic *American Top 40* radio show with Casey Kasem.

Reviews Make A Difference

YOUR VOICE COUNTS

Your review can make a huge difference. If you enjoyed this book, please consider giving it an honest review on Amazon. Thank you for your consideration.

R. Scott Murphy's Amazon Author Site

Made in the USA
Middletown, DE
23 May 2020